The rent veils
at Calvary

The rent veils
at Calvary

IAN R. K. PAISLEY

AMBASSADOR
Belfast • Greenville

The rent veils *at Calvary*

ISBN   1 898787 34 4

AMBASSADOR PRODUCTIONS LTD,
Providence House
16 Hillview Avenue,
Belfast, BT5 6JR
Northern Ireland

Emerald House,
1 Chick Springs Road, Suite 206
Greenville,
South Carolina 29609
United States of America

Foreword

This is not a book of writings but a book of speakings.

Its contents are not the written word but the spoken word.

It is a book of the preached Word of God.

No attempt has been made to recast its messages into literary form.

Its power rests not in the words which man's wisdom teacheth but in the power and demonstration of the Holy Spirit of God.

Preaching requires three ingredients - Truth, Clarity and Passion. These ingredients characterise the book.

Those who heard these sermons delivered requested their publication. May God set His seal upon them.

Ian R. K. Paisley

Eph 6:19 + 20

Martyrs Memorial Church, Belfast
March, 1997

Contents

The FIRST VEIL Christ rent at Calvary
the veil of darkness 9

The SECOND VEIL Christ rent at Calvary
the veil of separation 17

The THIRD VEIL Christ rent at Calvary
the veil of death 27

The FOURTH VEIL Christ rent at Calvary
the veil of the temple 35

The FIFTH VEIL Christ rent at Calvary
the veil of the rocks and earth (part one) 43

The FIFTH VEIL Christ rent at Calvary
the veil of the rocks and earth (part two) 51

The SIXTH VEIL Christ rent at Calvary
the veil of the graves 59

The SEVENTH VEIL Christ rent at Calvary
the veil of His flesh (part one) 69

The SEVENTH VEIL Christ rent at Calvary
the veil of His flesh (part two) 77

Appendix one

THE BLOOD AND WATER 87

Appendix two

THE POWER OF THE BLOOD 91

The FIRST VEIL Christ rent at Calvary
the veil of darkness

SCRIPTURE READING ~ MARK 15: 22-41

"And they bring him unto the place Golgotha, which is, being inter-preted, The place of a skull. And they gave him to drink wine min-gled with myrrh: but he received it not. And when they had crucified him, they parted his garments, casting lots upon them, what every man should take. And it was the third hour, and they crucified him. And the superscription of his accusation was written over, THE KING OF THE JEWS. And with him they crucify two thieves; the one on his right hand, and the other on his left. And the scripture was fulfilled, which saith, And he was numbered with the transgressors. And they that passed by railed on him, wagging their heads, and saying, Ah, thou that destroyest the temple, and buildest it in three days. Save thyself, and come down from the cross. Likewise also the chief priests mocking said among themselves with the scribes, He saved others; himself he cannot save. Let Christ the King of Israel descend now from the cross, that we may see and believe. And they that were cru-cified with him reviled him. And when the sixth hour was come, there was darkness over the whole land until the ninth hour. And at the ninth hour Jesus cried with a loud voice, saying, Eloi, Eloi, lama sabachthani? which is, being interpreted, My God, my God, why hast thou forsaken me? And some of them that stood by, when they heard

it, said, Behold, he called Elias. And one ran and filled a sponge full
of vinegar, and put it on a reed, and gave him to drink, saying, Let
alone; let us see whether Elias will come to take him down. And
Jesus cried with a loud voice, and gave up the ghost. And the veil of
the temple was rent in twain from the top to the bottom. And when
the centurion, which stood over against him, saw that he so cried
out, and gave up the ghost, he said, Truly this man was the Son of
God. There were also women looking on afar off: among whom was
Mary Magdalene, and Mary the mother of James the less and of Joses,
and Salome; (Who also, when he was in Galilee, followed him, and
ministered unto him;) and many other women which came up with
him unto Jerusalem."

God will stamp with His own divine seal of approval and blessing this reading from His very own Infallible Book.

I want to commence a short series of messages upon the Cross of our Lord
Jesus Christ under the title "The Seven Veils Which Christ Rent At Calvary".

Turning to Mark's Gospel chapter 15 and verse 38 we read, "and the veil of
the temple was rent in twain from the top to the bottom". The cross of our Lord
Jesus Christ is the centre and also the circumference of the whole Bible revelation. It is the exclusive hallmark of Biblical Christianity. A Crossless Christianity is
not Christianity at all. Without the Gospel of the Cross the Gospel does not exist.
It is a useless thing without power and without hope.

Look with me for a moment at some scriptures. I Corinthians 1:18 "For the
preaching of the cross is to them that perish foolishness; but unto us which are
saved it is the power of God." Turn over to the second chapter of the same 1st
Corinthian letter and the verse two "For I determined not to know any thing
among you, save Jesus Christ, and him crucified." Turn over to the fifteenth chapter of the same 1st Corinthian letter and the verse three "For I delivered unto you
first of all that which I also received, how that Christ died for our sins according to
the scriptures".

THE CROSSLESS GOSPEL

Since modern thought, so called, has come into twentieth century Christianity the organised established churches of the land are engaged in the outra-

geous business of forgetting that the Cross is the centre and circumference of the Gospel. They have adulterated the Gospel with the wisdom of man. They have blurred its great central truth of the shedding of the Saviour's blood upon the Cross. They have drained the Gospel of Blood until the message they present is anaemic and therefore lifeless and powerless.

"Back to the Cross" must be the clarion call of the true soldiers of Christ in this twentieth century apostasy. Without apology, without compromise and without delay we must re-erect the Cross. We must uplift and proclaim Jesus Christ and Him crucified.

The amazing thing is this, that every time you lift your Bible and you read the record of the Cross and its history you will be amazed at the glorious freshness of that wondrous scene and the gracious newness that is always revealed by its contemplation.

There are a whole series of sevens at the Cross. Seven in Scripture is the number of perfection and the perfection of all perfections is found at the cross.

You will remember the seven cries that Jesus uttered from the Cross. You may not know, but seven miracles were performed at the Cross. Many years ago, just after this building was opened, I preached a series of messages on the seven cries from the Cross and the seven miracles that were done at the Cross. I understand the tapes of those messages are still available.

If you look carefully at the Cross you will find seven groups of identified and named persons.

Recently when I was in Toronto my good friend and brother Dr Rod Bell preached a powerful message upon the things that Christ touched at Calvary. As I was looking at the portion of Scripture concerning the Cross as he preached, something jumped out of the page at me. It was the word "rent". The veil of the temple was rent. Then the rocks were rent. I knew I was onto a line of thought that would be most profitable and helpful and I discovered that there were seven veils rent at Calvary.

RENDING THE VEIL OF DARKNESS

I want to talk to you about the first one, which is the rending of the veil of darkness. If you look at that passage in Mark's Gospel you will find that Mark gives us the timing of the Cross and that is of vital importance. Just check with me that portion in the fifteenth chapter of Mark which we read together. When was

Christ crucified? At what hour was He put upon the cross? It was the third hour, verse 25, "and they crucified him". That was nine o'clock in the morning, our time.

Then come down the chapter and you will see something else. Verse 33," and when the sixth hour was come there was darkness over the whole land until the ninth hour". That was from twelve until three o'clock in the afternoon. Those hours are very important. You ask me why. Because at the Temple every morning there was the morning sacrifice of the lamb. What time did it take place? It took place at nine o'clock. God's Lamb upon the Cross was crucified at nine in the morning. Because He is the fulfiller of the blessed type of the morning sacrifice. What time in the evening was the offering made? There was a morning lamb and there was an evening lamb. It was exactly at three o'clock in the afternoon that the evening lamb was offered.

Jesus Christ is not only the Morning Sacrifice but, praise God, He is the Evening Sacrifice. He has fulfilled all the types and shadows of the Cross connected with the whole ritual of Mosaic Judaism. So everything is important.

THE MIRACLE DARKNESS

But something happened at the sixth hour, that was at midday. When the sixth hour was come there was darkness over the whole land. Did it last until Jesus died? No. It only lasted until the ninth hour, until three o'clock.

When you go home check the parallel passages in the Gospel of Luke and in the Gospel of Matthew.

This darkness was of course a miracle darkness. Think of it. Half the world was in darkness but at the sixth hour the other half of the world was suddenly plunged into darkness, and the first time since creation that this whole earth was in darkness took place at Calvary. The modern translations say it was an eclipse of the sun. An eclipse of the sun only lasts for a few minutes. This darkness lasted for three hours. In fact, no eclipse of the sun can ever take place when there is a full moon and there was always a full moon at the Passover.

This darkness reminds us of the first creation. The second verse of the Bible says "The earth was without form and void". Interesting, the word that was used there was "darkness over all the earth". In the other passages that run parallel with Mark's record, "Darkness was upon the face of the deep. And the Spirit of

God moved upon the face of the waters." Entire darkness. Not just darkness on one part of the world but on it all.

THE NIGHT OF GOD'S WRATH

Notice also that this darkness was wrapped in its central place around the cross. Light fights with darkness and dispels it. But here was a darkness that extinguished the light of the world. Here was a darkness that conquered. What darkness is this? This is a darkness which is divine. This is a darkness which signifies the awful wrath, the awful judgment, the awful curse of God. In these three hours Jesus Christ faced the darkness of my hell, the darkness of my damnation, the waves and billows of the darkness of the everlasting hell that I deserve because of my sins was poured down upon the head of the Son of God.

The darkness that the elect would all have received in the everlasting caverns of the damned in the blackness of darkness for ever, concentrated on the Light of the World while He hung upon that Cross. This darkness did not come on by twilight and then by increasing darkness until it was completely fulfilled in its intensity. No, it was an intense darkness from the beginning. Before this darkness came there was action at the Cross. The Lord Jesus was active. He prayed that great prayer "Father forgive them for they know not what they do". He had a conversation with Mary His mother, and with John His beloved disciple. He said "Woman behold thy son, son behold thy mother". Words of grace came from His lips when He said to the dying thief "Today thou shalt be with me in paradise".

SILENCING DARKNESS

Then He was silent when the darkness came. Before the darkness evil men taunted Him, the priests reviled Him, the crowds mocked Him and the people jeered at Him. But when the darkness came they were silent. Not a word was spoken when this awful darkness fell. This was the most frightening darkness that ever came upon this world. It was like the darkness that came down in a limited manner in Egypt when there was such a thick darkness that it could be felt, and no man rose from his bed or spoke one to the other for three days.

But for three hours this world was hung with the curtains of God's eternal wrath and behind those curtains, in the secret place, God drew His sword of justice and plunged it into the bosom of His well beloved Son.

O Christ, what burdens bowed Thy head!
Our load was laid on Thee;
Thou stoodest in the sinner's stead,
Didst bear all ill for me.
A victim led, Thy blood was shed;
Now there's no load for me.

Death and the curse were in our cup:
O Christ, 'twas full for Thee!
But Thou hast drained the last dark drop,
'Tis empty now for me:
That bitter cup, love drank it up;
Now blessing's draught for me.

Jehovah lifted up His rod:
O Christ, it fell on Thee!
Thou wast sore stricken of Thy God;
There's not one stroke for me:
Thy tears, Thy blood beneath it flowed;
Thy bruising healeth me.

Jehovah bade His sword awake:
O Christ, it woke 'gainst Thee!
Thy blood the flaming blade must slake,
Thy heart its sheath must be:
All for my sake, my peace to make—
Now sleeps that sword for me.

CHRIST'S WORD RENT THIS VEIL

How long did this darkness, this intense darkness last? It lasted until Jesus spoke again. What rent the veil of this darkness? The same thing that rent the veil of the darkness in Genesis God said, "Let there be light". And when God spoke the darkness was finished. When the Son of God spoke He said a very unusual thing. The ninth hour came and He cried "My God, my God, why hast thou forsaken me".

Why did God forsake Him? Because He was our Surety. He had entered into a solemn obligation to be responsible for our debts as far as a broken law was concerned.

Why did God forsake Him? Because He was our Substitute, He stood in our place and where I should have stood to receive the whip of God's terror and torment, He stood in that place and took that whipping, that beating, that punishment, that hell for my soul.

Why was He forsaken? Because He was our Sin Bearer. He was forsaken because He was made sin for us, who knew no sin, that we might be made the righteousness of God in Him.

Why was He forsaken? Because He was our Sacrifice. The Lamb must die that others might live. The Lamb must be punished if others are to be pardoned.

You will notice immediately after He said this He cried again and said, "Father". The forsaking is finished. He started Calvary with the words "Father forgive them, they know not what they do" in unity with His Father. In the darkness He went out into that God-forsaken place. But in the ninth hour when He spoke the darkness disappeared forever, because He had done His work as our Surety, as our Substitute, as our Sin-bearer and as our Sacrifice.

THE TIMING OF THE LIGHT

At three o'clock, at the exact time when the priest was taking the evening sacrificial lamb and slaying it and when the blood was flowing, so praise God, the Saviour finished the work that God gave Him to do. But between the cry "Why hast thou forsaken me" and the cry "Into thy hands I commit my spirit" was one other cry. It was the cry "Finished".

The work was done.

Jesus paid it all,
All to Him I owe.
Sin had left a crimson stain,
He washed it white as snow.

There was a veil rent at Calvary. It was the veil of darkness. It will never be sewn up again. That darkness will never, never return to me because God has said "Let there be light," and praise God, He has brought life and immortality to light through the Gospel.

I picked up an old book yesterday and I was touched with the words of a hymn which was quoted therein:

"I see the crowd in Pilate's hall,
I mark their wrathful mein,
Their shouts of "crucify" appal
With blasphemy between.
And of that shouting multitude
I feel that I am one,
And in that din of voices rude
I recognised my own.
T'was I that shed His sacred blood,
I nailed Him to the tree,
I crucified the Christ of God,
I joined the mockery.
Yet not the less that blood avails
To cleanse away my sin,
And not the less that cross prevails
To give me peace within."

He has made peace for us by the blood of His Cross. Do you know anything about it? Have you had the experience? Are you born again? Are you a blood washed child of heaven? If you are not, let me invite you and tell you there is room at the Cross for you. Wash, wash, and be clean.

AMEN AND AMEN

The SECOND VEIL Christ rent at Calvary
the veil of separation

SCRIPTURE READINGS

MATTHEW 27:38-44

"Then were there two thieves crucified with him, one on the right hand, and another on the left. And they that passed by reviled him, wagging their heads, And saying, Thou that destroyest the temple, and buildest it in three days, save thyself. If thou be the Son of God, come down from the cross. Likewise also the chief priests mocking him, with the scribes and elders, said, he saved others; himself he cannot save. If he be the King of Israel, let him now come down from the cross, and we will believe him. He trusted in God, let him deliver him now, if he will have him: for he said, I am the Son of God. The thieves also, which were crucified with him, cast the same in his teeth."

MARK 15: 27-32

"And with him they crucify two thieves; the one on his right hand, and the other on his left. And the scripture was fulfilled, which saith, And he was numbered with the transgressors. And they that passed by railed on him, wagging their heads, and saying, Ah, thou that destroyest the temple, and buildest it in three days, Save thyself, and

come down from the cross. Likewise also the chief priests mocking said among themselves with the scribes, He saved others; himself he cannot save. Let Christ the King of Israel descend now from the cross, that we may see and believe. And they that were crucified with him reviled him. "

LUKE 23: 33-43

"And when they were come to the place, which is called Calvary, there they crucified him, and the malefactors, one on the right hand, and the other on the left. Then said Jesus, Father, forgive them; for they know not what they do. And they parted his raiment, and cast lots. And the people stood beholding. And the rulers also with them derided him, saying, he saved others; let him save himself, if he be Christ, the chosen of God. And the soldiers also mocked him, coming to him, and offering him vinegar, And saying, If thou be the king of the Jews, save thyself. And a superscription also was written over him in letters of Greek, and Latin, and Hebrew, THIS IS THE KING OF THE JEWS. And one of the malefactors which were hanged railed on him, saying, If thou be Christ, save thyself and us. But the other answering rebuked him, saying, Dost not thou fear God, seeing thou art in the same condemnation. And we indeed justly; for we receive the due reward of our deeds: but this man hath done nothing amiss. And he said unto Jesus, Lord, remember me when thou comest into thy kingdom. And Jesus said unto him, Verily I say unto thee, To day shalt thou be with me in paradise. And it was about the sixth hour, and there was a darkness over all the earth until the ninth hour."

JOHN 19: 17-18

"And he bearing his cross went forth into a place called the place of a skull, which is called in the Hebrew Golgotha: Where they crucified him, and two other with him, on either side one, and Jesus in the midst."

Our first study was the rending of the veil of darkness - the three hours of intense and terrible darkness on the Cross. The Lord Jesus rent that veil of darkness.

We come now to the second veil which was rent - the veil of separation demonstrated in the conversion of the dying thief.

Seven hundred years before Jesus died on Calvary the prophet Isaiah put on record the eternal decree of the everlasting God of heaven.

What was that decree? "He was numbered with the transgressors." That was seven hundred years before Calvary, but it was absolutely accurate and was indeed the voice and word of the God who cannot lie.

WRITTEN IN THE PAST TENSE

Notice, although it was seven hundred years before it cameto pass, it was written in the past tense. Isaiah did not say "he *will be* numbered with the transgressors". He said "he *was* numbered with the transgressors".

Why did the prophet use the past tense? He used the past tense because when God speaks it is as certain as if it had already taken place. The prophet was sure that Christ would be numbered with the transgressors.

What a wonder! The Lawgiver dying and numbered with the law breakers. That God's Christ, should be executed and die with godless criminals, and that the lawful Son of God should be hung up with men of lawlessness and men of sin!

But that was God's order. That was God's ordination. That was God's decree. What God has ordered and what God has ordained and what God has decreed, must come to pass.

He who was born among the beasts of the stable, was to die associated with the beasts and dregs of society.

THE THREE REASONS

There were three reasons for that.

Firstly, to mark the descent of shame into which Christ must go in order to save sinners.

Secondly, the definition of substitution which lies at the very heart of the message of the Gospel of salvation.

Christ must be numbered amongst transgressors. He must take their place. He must associate Himself with them. He must be crucified with two malefactors, two criminals, two thieves.

They were sinners indeed, but on the centre cross there was One who was made sin itself. There was One who was reckoned to be the criminal of all criminals, the sinner of all sinners for He was made sin for us.

Oh the wonder, that the pure and holy and spotless and impeccable Son of God should be made sin for me!

There we have the definition of substitution.

Thirdly, the distinction of God's Sovereignty.

God is sovereign and God's salvation is a sovereign work. In the salvation of men there is a division. There are sinners who go to hell and there are sinners who go to heaven.

How? By their own efforts? No. By their own good works? No. By their own religious deeds? No. By their own sacrifices? No. They go to heaven by the grace of God alone.

There is no story in all the Bible which magnifies free grace and free grace alone, like the story of the dying thief whom the Lord saved from the jaws of hell.

Charles Haddon Spurgeon, the greatest English preacher of all time and one of the greatest defenders of the faith in the Victorian era of Britain's life, said this:

"There stands a text, and I believe that it is my Father's wish that all men should be saved and to come to the knowledge of the truth. But I know also that He does not will that so that He will save any one of them unless they believe in His Son. He has told us over and over again that He will save no man except that man believes in His Son.

"Believing in the Son means a forsaking of sins and a turning to God with full purpose of heart. I know also that God has a people He will save, whom by His eternal love He has chosen and whom by His eternal power He will deliver. I do not know how that squares with this and other texts but I believe them all and I preach them all. There is a great truth - God's sovereignty.

There is also another truth - man's responsibility. It is my business not to try and reconcile them but to preach them as they stand in the Book."

So in this wonderful story of the salvation of the dying thief we have one of the greatest testimonies to the mighty distinction of God's absolute sovereignty in saving men.

THE DYING THIEF'S PRAYER

First note that this prayer which the thief offered was a prayer against all the circumstances that surrounded him.

You see this thief, this malefactor, this criminal, had also carried his cross. Jesus Christ, bearing the weight of the world's sin, had to have assistance to carry His cross. They compelled a man to carry it for Him. So as this thief walked he saw the weakness of Christ. You say, "How do I know Christ was weak?" Because the Holy Spirit tells me. He says "He was crucified through weakness." Only the Holy Spirit would dare to write such a word about Him who is the omnipotent God. Crucified through weakness.

That dying thief saw Christ was weak as He went to the cross. He saw Christ was weak as He was nailed to the cross. He saw Christ was weak as He hung upon that cross.

But something happened, grace touched miraculously, supernaturally, the heart of that thief and he prayed for the Saviour crucified through weakness to extend to him the might of His power and save him. The circumstances were against it but grace laughs at impossibilities and cries, "it must, it shall be done".

MARK WHEN HE PRAYED

Secondly, notice that he cried before the mighty events of Calvary had taken place. He cried before the three hours of intense darkness came. He cried before Christ cried "It is finished". He cried before the veil of the temple was rent. He cried before the rocks were smashed and broken. He cried before the graves were opened. He cried before the Lord had committed Himself and His Spirit to His Father. He cried before the centurion had confessed that Christ was indeed the Son of God.

Before the mighty events took place this man was supernaturally changed and so changed that he cried, "Lord, remember me when thou comest into thy kingdom."

The circumstances surrounding his conversion were unfavourable. The greatest of all events of Calvary were not complete, but yet this dying thief made his cry for salvation.

Do you know why? A genuine conversion is the work of the Spirit of God in men's hearts, and the Spirit of God was working on that man's heart. The saving of that man has a lesson to teach us all, a twofold lesson - the depths of Christ's stooping grace, how low Christ will stoop to save sinners, and a demonstration of the heights of Christ's saving grace. He lifted this man from the very jaws of hell to the very embrace of heaven.

THE GREAT SEPARATION

I want you to notice how separated from Christ this man was. His separation was demonstrated in the manifestation of his sin. We were reading about that. This man reviled Christ as he hung on the cross. This man joined with others in the vilification and the mocking of the Son of God. He cast in Christ's teeth the very accusations of the Jewish people - "If thou be the Christ save thyself". He went further and said "Save thyself and us".

Here is a manifestation of a heart ruined, a heart corrupted, a heart debauched, a heart depraved, joining with others in mocking the Son of God.

We need all to learn the iniquity of our inmost souls. That dying thief is a perfect representative of every sinner, of you and of me. A slave to sin, sin pushes us into total separation from God. The leper, a type of sinner, is cast out of the camp. His upper lip is covered and he cries "Unclean, unclean".

Here was a man as unclean as sin could make him, with jibes and blasphemy upon his lips concerning the Christ of God Who was hanging dying beside him in order that he might be saved. His separation is demonstrated in the manifestation of his sin.

This separation,, secondly, is demonstrated by his identification with already condemned sinners. Where did this dying thief place himself? Notice the great contrast in the words. He says to his partner in crime "We indeed justly but this man hath done nothing amiss". This man's separation is demonstrated not only in the manifestation of his sin but it is demonstrated in his identification with already condemned sinners in the same condemnation.

Until we take our place and identify ourselves with the mass of sinners there is no pardon for our souls and the veil of separation will remain unbroken. It can only be rent when we acknowledge that we are identified with the worst of sinners and cry out with Paul "I am the chief of sinners".

This separation is further demonstrated by his affirmation of the purity of the Saviour. He suddenly says "This man has done nothing amiss." All around this cross are sinners, religious sinners, chief priests and scribes, cursing the Saviour.

Barbarous sinners, the soldiers who mocked him and drove the nails through His hands and feet and lifted Him up on that cross, the old tree of the cross of shame. Now we, in the same condemnation, we too are sinners of the vilest order, but this Man has done nothing amiss.

WANTED THE SINLESS MAN

The sinner is only saved when he finds One who has no sin. For everyone stained by sin is impotent in the salvation of either themselves or any of their fellows. We must find a sinless person.

Let me go further, it is not enough to find a sinless God, we must find a sinless Man. We must find One who is part and parcel of the human race. We must find One who has become bone of our bone and flesh of our flesh. If this great gulf that fixed us into separation because of sin has to be bridged, it must be bridged by One who is truly the perfect God of heaven and just as truly the perfect Man of earth.

Blessed be God that is what Jesus is. "This Man has done nothing amiss."

This separation is also demonstrated in the dying thief's recognition of the fear of God.

Did you notice what he said to his companion? The one that he a few moments before had joined with in rebuking and reviling and jibing and mocking the Lord Jesus. He said "Dost thou not fear God?"

A moment before it he did not fear God but, listen, the fear of God is the beginning of wisdom. The Holy Spirit had started the work upon his heart. When the Holy Spirit starts to work upon a man's heart the fear of God is the first-fruits. It is the first-fruits of the work of the Spirit of God.

Into this man's tormented mind and heart there came this word. Can my separation be brought to an end?

Can this dreadful veil which separates me from all that is good and pure and godly be rent?

Can the great partition between my soul and God be swept away?

Can the great gulf fixed be bridged?

Can I, who now am in separation as a sinner, and dying and going out to hell, can I suddenly be incorporated to be a companion - not of my fellow criminal, but of this Holy, Spotless, Sinless Man who dies beside me? Oh, what a work of grace was taking place in this man's heart!

MARK THE WORDS HE USES

Notice also the words that he uses. This man is in the same condemnation. We are coming now to the heart of the Gospel, because the heart of the Gospel is this - that Jesus stood in the same condemnation as sinners, that He was Himself the representative of sinners.

Into that man's mind came that question - why, why, why is this holy man in the same place of condemnation as myself and my fellow companion in crime? The Holy Spirit was teaching him the truth.

You see this man was a Jew, he was not a Gentile.

You say, "How do you know?" Because a Gentile knew nothing about Christ. This man had already taken up the charge - "if thou be the Christ save thyself and us".

He was a Jew. He understood. But there was something more. He not only took part in the language employed by the priests in vilifying our Lord but he read something.

You will notice in all the passages we read that the Kingship of Christ was challenged. The priests challenged it, the thieves challenged it. Go back and read it carefully, above His head there was this word, THIS IS JESUS, THE KING OF THE JEWS. There are two things which bring a man to Christ, the fear of God and the word of God.

You will notice too that there were the modern translators of God's Word at the cross. They went to Pilate and said, "We want that changed, we don't like that. We don't like that pure testimony to Christ. You have got to write in 'He said He was king of the Jews'".

Old Pilate smiled and he said "The authorised version stands. It stands. It will not be altered".

It was the word of God.

Where is He that is born king of the Jews? Into the darkened mind of that criminal on the cross there shone the light of the Word - This man is the king. If He is the king he can do all things. He can even save me, a wretch of hell.

So he cries and says, "Lord" the word for God. The sinner knows that the only person who can save him must be God incarnate. The Christ of the unitarian, the Christ of the modernist, the Christ of 20th century apostasy cannot save anyone. The only Christ who can save is the Christ of the New Testament and He is God manifest in the flesh. "Lord, remember me when thou comest into thy kingdom." Thy kingdom, he recognised Him as the king.

NOTE THESE DIRECT PARALLELS

Now, in closing, I want you to open your Bible at Luke's Gospel and look with me at the testimony that occurs there. I only saw this last night as I was preparing this message concerning the death of the Lord Jesus. So we come over to Luke's Gospel and we come to what the dying thief said and what Jesus said, and there are direct parallels,

I want you to notice this, sentence by sentence.

First of all, the dying thief, it is recorded "And he said unto Jesus" and in parallel with that put these words "And Jesus said unto him". That is the first parallel.

Now we come to the second parallel in these verses. "He said Lord," and the Lord said "Verily, I say unto thee". When he said "Lord" he acknowledged that he was praying to the God of truth. Luke chapter 23 and verses 42 and 43 "Verily I say unto you". "Verily" is "truth" - truly I say unto you.

Then the dying thief said something more. He said "remember me". The parallel in the next verse is "Thou shalt be with me". "Remember me," that was his prayer, but the Lord Jesus said "Thou shalt be with me."

Then the dying thief said "remember me when thou comest into thy kingdom". The parallel to that in the word of Christ is "Today". The thief said "when you come into your kingdom remember me". The Lord Jesus Christ said "you are going to be with me and it is going to happen today, not in the millennium or not in the eternal age but today you are going to be with Me".

He wanted to be with Him in the kingdom but Jesus gave him something far better than that. Today thou shalt be with me, where? in paradise, in the paradise of God.

BACK TO GENESIS

Go back to Genesis, to the paradise where Adam and Eve were. They fell and were cast out and there was a flaming sword which kept the way to the tree of life, and no one was in that garden but God alone. All mankind was separated and that garden remained a testimony on earth until the flood, and then God transferred that garden to heaven. That is where it is today.

You can read about it where the tree of life grows in heaven, it is the same tree of life transplanted to heaven.

It is coming back again, of course, because when God transfers the city He is going to bring paradise back and men are going to dwell in a new heaven and a new earth and paradise will be back. No one but God walked in the garden after the fall. The Lord Jesus said "I am rending the veil. I am taking away the barrier, dying thief, you are going to be with me in paradise. You are going to be in my company in paradise". What a rending of the veil it was!

JC Ryle has a wonderful sermon in one of his books, I would advise you to get it and read it. It is entitled " Christ's greatest trophy". He pictures Christ appearing at the Father's right hand and beside Him is a glorious friend, the spirit of the dying thief. And angels look and stare and say to Christ "Who is this that accompanies You? Who is this who is in step with You? Who is this who walks beside You, Your closest companion and courtier? Oh, King of kings, tell us who this is?"

Jesus says "This is a poor vile sinner, whom I shed My blood for and he is the firstfruits of a great multitude which no man can number out of every kingdom and race and creed, and out of every colour. They are all coming and they are going to walk with Me and talk with Me and dwell with Me and sit in my throne with Me and reign with Me."

And the angels around stood aghast as they saw that bright spirit linked eternally with the Son of God in His glory.

Heavenly Father we thank thee for the sweetness and blessedness of Your Word.

AMEN AND AMEN!

The THIRD VEIL Christ rent at Calvary
the veil of death

SCRIPTURE READING ~ JOHN 19:28-42

"After this, Jesus knowing that all things were now accomplished that the scripture might be fulfilled, saith, I thirst. Now there was set a vessel full of vinegar: and they filled a spunge with vinegar, and put it upon hyssop, and put it to his mouth. When Jesus therefore had received the vinegar, he said, it is finished: and he bowed his head, and gave up the ghost. The Jews therefore, because it was the preparation, that the bodies should not remain upon the cross on the sabbath day, (for that sabbath day was an high day,) besought Pilate that their legs might be broken, and that they might be taken away. Then came the soldiers, and brake the legs of the first, and of the other which was crucified with him. But when they came to Jesus, and saw that he was dead already, they brake not his legs: But one of the soldiers with a spear pierced his side, and forthwith came there out blood and water. And he that saw it bare record, and his record is true: and he knoweth that he saith true, that ye might believe. For these things were done, that the scripture should be fulfilled, A bone of him shall not be broken. And again another scripture saith, They shall look on him whom they pierced. And after this Joseph of Arimithaea, being a disciple of Jesus, but secretly for fear of the Jews, besought Pilate that he might take away the body of Jesus: and Pilate

*gave him leave. He came therefore, and took the body of Jesus. And
there came also Nicodemus, which at the first came to Jesus by night,
and brought a mixture of myrrh and aloes, about an hundred pound
weight. Then took they the body of Jesus, and wound it in linen clothes
with the spices, as the manner of the Jews is to bury. Now in the place
where he was crucified there was a garden; and in the garden a
new sepulchre, wherein was never man yet laid. There laid they Jesus therefore because of the Jews' preparation day; for the sepulchre
was night at hand."*

We have been considering the rent veils at the cross. We discovered that
the Saviour rent the veil of darkness at the end of three hours. There are deep
spiritual lessons to be learned from the rending of that veil of darkness.

We discovered that for the dying thief He rent the veil of separation. What
a wonderful story that is, of the triumph of free and sovereign grace.

This morning we want to consider the rending of the veil of death.

DEATH THE GREAT PUTTER OUT

What a veil death has spread all over this old sinful world of ours, in all
generations of man's history. Death puts out the light and leaves sinners in darkness. Death slays the hope that burns within the human breast and leaves the
sinners in a state of hopelessness. Death incarcerates the sinner in bondage and
lays upon fallen mankind that bondage which prevails during the whole of their
lifetime on earth, described in the words of Scripture "all their lifetime subject to
bondage". That is the curse of sin, continual bondage, day in and day out in all the
years of life's existence. Death is the last great enemy with which we must all fight
our last fight, for death is the righteous judgment of God fulfilled upon the
sinner. Did not God say to our first parents "In the day that thou eatest of the
forbidden fruit, thou shalt surely die", and die we will and die we must.

SIN FINDS SINNERS OUT

God does and will foreclose upon sinners in judgment. The sinner is duped.
The prohibition of paradise, "the day that thou eatest thereof thou shalt
surely die, Thou shalt not eat of the tree of knowledge of good and evil". That

prohibition is complemented with the warning, "Be sure your sins will find you out". Eat of this tree, Adam and Eve, and your sin will find you out. As our first parents took of the fruit of that tree and ate of it what happened? Their glorious garments suddenly dissolved and they stood in stark shameful nakedness before their Maker. Their sin had found them out. I hear Adam and Eve cry out "Our sin has found us out". For the first time they had learned what it was to be in a terrible fear of God. Never before had fear shaken their sinless souls. But now that their souls were sinful, fear, the terror of an avenging righteous God, fell upon them. Their sin was finding them out.

"Our sin has found us out," they shrieked as they took the fig leaves and stitched them hastily together to find a covering for their shame. "Our sins have found us out," they wailed as they ran for cover to hide themselves among the trees of the garden. "Our sins have found us out," as they shook and trembled and heard the voice of the Lord God walking in the garden and crying out "Where art thou?" Sin, their sin, had found them out. They learned that pay-day certainly came, and pay-day will certainly come to us all.

HOW SIN IS FINISHED

There is a day when sin is finished and how is it finished? "By one man sin entered into the world and death by sin, and sin, when it is finished, bringeth forth death." The fruit, the finished, the final fruit of sin is death, final, full separation from the God of heaven in hell's flames and torments for evermore. "Whosoever was not found written in the Book of Life was cast into the lake of fire. This is the second death."

That dark veil of the doom and damnation of death was rent at Calvary by our Lord Jesus Christ. Seven times the Saviour spoke on the cross. Three times He addressed His speech to God. "Father, forgive them, they know not what they do". "My God, my God, why hast thou forsaken me?" "Father, into thy hands I commend my spirit." Three cries from the cross were cries to God.

Three cries from the cross were addressed to men. The cry of Christ to the dying thief "Today thou shalt be with me in paradise". The cry from the cross to John "Behold thy mother" and to Mary "Behold thy son". These are the cries that came from the cross. Then there was another cry addressed to all the spectators "I thirst". There was one cry on the cross which was different from all the rest. It was addressed to all who could hear. It was addressed to the Father, it was addressed to the Holy Spirit of God. It was addressed to all mankind of all ages, to souls already dead and souls doomed to die in coming generations. It was addressed to the fowls of the air, the beasts of the field and the fishes of the sea. It was addressed to all created things both in heaven and in earth. It was addressed to angels and archangels and cherubims and seraphims. It was addressed to all. It is the cry that we have here in this portion of Scripture which we read together. The nineteenth chapter of John's Gospel and at the verse 30 "When Jesus therefore had received the vinegar, he said, It is finished." In the Greek text that is one word not three words. It is the word "Finished", the word spoken by Christ to the Father, to the Holy Ghost, to all heaven, to all earth and to all hell. Finished.

LEARNING THE MEANING OF "FINISHED"

That is a most interesting word. That word occurs twelve times in the New Testament. If you have a pencil you should note these occurrences. I must go over them very quickly. The first one is in Matthew 13:53 where we read "When Jesus had *finished* these parables". That word finished is this word which came from Christ's lips in that great cry from the cross addressed to all who could hear and all who would hear. Matthew 19:1 "Jesus had finished these sayings". That is the same word.

Matthew 26:1 "Jesus had *finished* all these sayings".

Then in our text in John 19:30 "It is *finished*".

In Acts 20:24 it is used by Paul "So that I might *finish* my course".

In Acts 21:7 "When we had *finished* our course from Tyre".

In II Timothy 4:17 "I have fought a good fight, I have *finished* my course".

In Hebrews 4:3 "The works were *finished* from the foundation of the world".

In Revelation 10:7 "The mystery of God is finished". In Revelation 11:7 "When they shall have *finished* their testimony".

In Revelation 20:5 "Until the thousand years were *finished*". Revelation 20:7 "The thousand years *expire*" - that is the same word.

THE REAL MEANING

If you put all those texts together you will find the real meaning of this word. It is the bringing to a total end. It is the finishing of a life's work. It is the completion of a journey. It is the achieving of a goal. It is the fulfilment of Divine purpose. It is the final act of testimony. It is the ending of an epoch. It is an achievement of a goal within the time limits. It is the finishing of a preordained work and it is the finality of death. If you put together those twelve references to that word, you will get the real meaning of this word "finished".

Twelve, of course, in Scripture is a perfect number. It is the perfection of Divine government. The whole government that God ordered for men is stamped with the number twelve. There were twelve patriarchs from Seth to Noah. There were twelve patriarchs from Shem to Jacob, Jacob's sons, twelve patriarchs making up the tribes of Israel. That is government in the pre-Israelite times and in the Israelite times, covering the whole of the Old Testament.

The New Testament apostolic government twelve apostles. When we come to the eternal age it is characterised by a city that has twelve foundations, that has twelve gates, that has twelve pearls as gates and angels standing as sentinels at each of the gates. At the heart of the cross is the Divine government. At the heart of the cross is the battle for supremacy and sovereignty of that government. At the heart of the cross is this greatest of all governmental questions "Shall death rule, for death had conquered life in the fall of Eden. Shall that death continue to rule or shall life conquer death? Can fallen paradise be regained? Can the way of access to the tree of life be regained for man?" That is the great question that lies at the heart of this cry. When Jesus Christ cried "It is finished" He was bringing His whole grand and glorious work of redemption to a final and total completion. As He went to the cross He said, "I have a baptism to be baptised of and how am I straightened until it be accomplished (or finished)." So at the heart of this cry is this thought of bringing it to an end.

THE END OF THE JOURNEY

Also it is the end of a journey. Why did Jesus journey into this world? He came to seek and to save that which was lost. It is the finishing of a life work. Standing before Pilate He cried, "For this end I was born". It is the achieving of a goal, "For this purpose, He said, came I into the world." It is the final act of testimony. "If I be lifted up, He said, I will draw all unto me." If you look at your testament you will find the word "men" is in italics, it is not in the Greek text. At the cross Jesus Christ drew all to him.

Every devil in hell was at the cross to destroy Him, but He was uplifted. He drew the powers of hell and we read in Colossians chapter two that He triumphed over them in His cross, stripping off from Himself principalities and powers.

When He was uplifted He drew to the cross all sinful men and every type and character of sinful man is depicted in the characters around the cross. Religious men, priests and scribes, political men, the rulers of the people and military men, the soldiers around the cross.

But He drew to Him at the cross the wrath of the Infinite God of heaven. "All thy waves and thy billows rolled over Me."

It is the finishing of a preordained work. He said, "I come to do thy will O my God." He knelt as He sweat His blood in dark Gethsemane and said "Not my will but thine be done." It is the attaining of a set goal. What was His goal? What was the first word that Jesus is recorded to have spoken as a boy of twelve? "I must be about my Father's business". What was this great cry? It was the finishing of the Father's business. "I have finished the work that thou hast given me to do." It is the ending of an era and what an era ended here. "Once He appeared," Paul tells us in the Hebrew epistle, "in the end of the age to put away sin by the sacrifice of Himself". When He put away sin a new era began, the era of Gospel grace and the light that was limited in Old Testament times rose to meridian across the world as He said "Go and preach to every creature this Gospel".

DEATH'S OBITUARY

Of course, it was the finality of death. For after He cried this word He said "Father into thy hands I commend my spirit". I want you to notice something else about this word from the cross, it is the only loud voiced cry of Christ. All the other Scriptures that we read we do not read that He cried loudly. But when we read about this particular voice, you find it in Luke's Gospel 23:46. It is a very important word, tt says "And when Jesus had cried with a loud voice" He said, He did not cry, "Father into thy hands I commend my spirit." After He had cried with a loud voice. What was the cry immediately before He said "Father into thy hands I commend my spirit". It was this cry "It is finished". It is the only word from the cross in which the volume is specially mentioned by the Holy Spirit in the Scriptural record, this great cry from the cross.

This cry marks the death of death itself. It was Christ who shouted here. Death did not shout for at the cross death itself was silenced forever, for the cross is the destruction of death and the cross is the defeat of death. The cross is the sepulchre of our sins and it is the grave of death. The death of deaths and the sepulchre of sin is found here in this cry of Christ.

Turn with me to Hebrews chapter two and there you have this truth set forth in the plainest possible way. Hebrews 2:14-15 "But as much then as the children are partakers of flesh and blood, He also Himself likewise took part of the same; that through death He might destroy him that had the power of death, that is, the devil; and deliver them who through fear of death were all their lifetime subject to bondage." What happened? At the cross, Jesus Christ, when He cried "It is finished" tore asunder the veil of death itself. Mr Spurgeon said "This cry 'It is finished' consolidated heaven, shook hell, comforted earth, delighted the Father, glorified the Son, brought down the Holy Ghost, confirmed the everlasting covenant and saved all the elect and chosen people of God." So it did.

Finished, the work was forever done.

GADSBY'S HYMN BOOK

I was looking at Gadsby's old hymn-book this morning as I was meditating on this text in my study and I came to a great old hymn.

'Tis finished, the Messiah dies,
Cut off for sins but not His own,
Accomplished is the sacrifice
The great redeeming work is done.
Finished our vile transgression is,
And purged the guilt of all our sins,
And everlasting righteousness
Is bought for all His people in.
Tis finished, all my guilt and pain
I want no sacrifice beside.
For me, for me, the Lamb was slain,
And I'm forever justified.
Sin, death and hell are now subdued,
All grace is now to sinners given.
And lo I gleaned the atoning blood
For pardoned holiness and hell.

Finished - the work is done. Nothing can be taken from it. Nothing can be added to it.

Jesus paid it all.
All to Him I owe.
Sin had left a crimson stain,
 He washed it white as snow.

Dear sinner, wash and be clean. Dear backslider, return to that cross and be washed afresh in the precious blood. Dear believer, let your song forever be "Jesus keep me near the cross".

AMEN AND AMEN!

The FOURTH VEIL Christ rent at Calvary
the veil of the temple

SCRIPTURE READING ~ HEBREWS 9:1-28

"Then verily the first covenant had also ordinances of divine service, and a worldly sanctuary. For there was a tabernacle made; the first, wherein was the candlestick, and the table, and the shewbread; which is called the sanctuary. And after the second veil, the tabernacle which is called the Holiest of all; Which had the golden censer, and the ark of the covenant overlaid round about with gold, wherein was the golden pot that had manna and Aaron's rod that budded, and the tables of the covenant; And over it the cherubims of glory shadowing the mercyseat; of which we cannot now speak particularly. Now when these things were thus ordained, the priests went always into the first tabernacle, accomplishing the service of God. But into the second went the high priest alone once every year, not without blood, which he offered for himself, and for the errors of the people: The Holy Ghost this signifying that the way into the holiest of all was not yet made manifest, while as the first tabernacle was yet standing; Which was a figure for the time them present, in which were offered both gifts and sacrifices, that could not make him that did the service perfect, as pertaining to the conscience; Which stood only in meats and drinks, and divers washings, and carnal ordinances, imposed on them until the time of reformation. But Christ

being come an high priest of good things to come, by a greater and more perfect tabernacle, not made with hands, that is to say, not of this building; Neither by the blood of goats and calves, but by his own blood he entered in once into the holy place, having obtained eternal redemption for us. For if the blood of bulls and of goats, and the ashes of an heifer sprinkling the unclean, sanctifieth to the purifying of the flesh: How much more shall the blood of Christ, who through the eternal Spirit offered himself without spot to God, purge your conscience from dead works to serve the living God? And for this cause he is the mediator of the new testament, that by means of death, for the redemption of the transgressions that were under the first testament, they which are called might receive the promise of eternal inheritance. For where a testament is, there must also of necessity be the death of the testator. For a testament is of force after men are dead: otherwise it is of no strength at all while the testator liveth. Whereupon neither the first testament was dedicated without blood. For when Moses had spoken every precept to all the people according to the law, he took the blood of calves and of goats, with water, and scarlet wool, and hyssop and sprinkled both the book, and all the people. Saying, This is the blood of the testament which God hath enjoined unto you. Moreover he sprinkled with blood both the tabernacle, and all the vessels of the ministry. And almost all things are by the law purged with blood; and without shedding of blood is no remission. It was therefore necessary that the patterns of things in the heavens should be purified with these; but the heavenly things themselves with better sacrifices than these. For Christ is not entered into the holy places made with hands, which are the figures of the true; but into heaven itself, now to appear in the presence of God for us; Nor yet that she should offer himself often as the high priest entereth into the holy place every year with blood of others. For then must he often have suffered since the foundation of the world; but now once in the end of the world hath he appeared to put away sin by the sacrifice of himself. And as it is appointed unto men once to die, but after this the judgment; So Christ was once offered to bear the sins of many; and unto them that look for him shall he appear the second time without sin unto salvation."

We have been looking at a most interesting, instructive and intriguing subject - The Seven Veils Which Were Rent At Calvary.

We have looked at the veil of darkness which Jesus rent at the cross.

We have looked at the veil of separation which Jesus rent at the cross.

We have looked at the veil of death which Jesus rent at the cross.

We come now to look at the veil of the temple.

Some texts of Scripture, Matthew 27:50-51 *"Jesus, when he had cried again with a loud voice, yielded up the ghost. And, behold, the veil of the temple was rent in twain from the top to the bottom."* Mark 15: 37-38 *"And Jesus cried with a loud voice, and gave up the ghost. And the veil of the temple was rent in twain from the top to the bottom."* Luke 23: 45 *"And the sun was darkened, and the veil of the temple was rent in the midst. And when Jesus had cried with a loud voice, he said, Father, into thy hands I commend my spirit: and having said thus, he gave up the ghost."*

If you turn over to John's Gospel, and this is very important, chapter 19, you will find there the setting of the rending of that veil. John's Gospel 19:28 *"After this, Jesus knowing that all things were now accomplished, that the scripture might be fulfilled, said, I thirst. Now there was set a vessel full of vinegar: and they filled a spunge with vinegar, and put it upon hyssop, and put it to his mouth. When Jesus therefore had received the vinegar, he said, It is finished; and he bowed his head, and gave up the ghost."*

COMPARE AND SEE

If you lay those four Scriptures carefully beside one another and compare them you will find that the loud voice cry was the cry "It is finished".

Before and preceding His last prayer which was "Father, into thy hands I commend my spirit," the Gospel of Matthew, Mark and Luke all emphasise the loud voice preceding the dismissing of His spirit to His Father.

The cry was loud because it was for the world of devils to hear, the world of angels to hear, and the world of human beings to hear. His last words He said were for His Father's ear, "Father, into thy hands I commend my spirit."

So Matthew, Mark and Luke emphasise the strength of the cry - it was a loud cry. John instead emphasises the words "It is finished". The real significance of the rent veil hinges on the timing when this cry was made. Now the Mosaic form of worship was centred in a mercy seat where there always shone what was known as the Shekinah Glory.

During the wilderness sojourn of God's people that billow of light issued through the tent and the curtains and was a great light of cloud above the tabernacle during the day. It was a great ball of fire during the night. When it moved the congregation of Israel moved. When it stopped the congregation of Israel stopped.

THE PLACE OF THE MERCY SEAT

The mercy seat was in a sanctuary known in Scripture as the Holiest of all. Of course, the replica of that was found also in the temple of Solomon and the other temples which were built after the destruction of Solomon's Temple. Now the way to the mercy seat was blocked up and securely barricaded. In the outward court of the temple there was a place known as the Court of the Gentiles. If you and I had been living in that day that is as far as we would have got, to the outer court, the Court of the Gentiles.

That is what Ephesians chapter two means when it says "Ye that sometime were afar off are made nigh by the blood of Christ." Between the Court of the Gentiles and the sacred enclosure of the temple precincts there was a wall, and no Gentile was allowed to pass that wall. So the way into the holiest of all for Gentiles was securely blocked.

The next building was the Court of the Women. The women of Israel had a court of their own. It was beyond the wall of the Gentile Court but it too was divided from the temple area. There was the barricade of the wall for the Gentiles, the barricade of the steps for the women.

If you had passed over those steps you would have come to the Court of Israel and the Court of the Priests where males of the tribes of Israel had all access, the Court of Israel and the Court of the Priests. It surrounded the real temple area but it was barricaded off from that temple area as well.

Then there was the holy place. That contained, as we have already read in Hebrews, the table of shewbread, the golden candlestick and the altar of incense.

Every day priests of the tribe of Levi went into that holy place.

Beyond that holy place there was the Holiest of all. That was where the mercy seat was and the ark of the covenant. For the mercy seat was the lid of the ark of the covenant.

Only once a year could the high priest of Israel draw aside the great veil that reached from the ceiling of the temple to the floor, and pass through and when he passed through the curtain fell back into position.

He had to carry with him a basin of sacrificial blood. He had to offer that blood for himself as a sinner and for the errors and sins of the people. After he had done that he returned to the holy place.

Now these inhibitions must all be removed if you and I are going to be saved and cleansed from our sins. You must also remember that the temple and tabernacle were types of heaven and you have a perfect picture of heaven in the temple and in the tabernacle.

We were reading this morning in that great ninth chapter of Hebrews, and could I just refer you to verse 23 . "It was therefore necessary that the pattern of things in the heavens should be purified with these. But the heavenly things themselves with better sacrifices than these." So the tabernacle, the holy place, was but a type of what is in heaven. Of course, the way to God in heaven was blocked to us all. Our sins had separated between us and God.

THE WAY IN

Now turn with me to the third chapter of Genesis and verse 24, "So he drove out the man and he placed at the east of the garden of Eden cherubims and a flaming sword which turned every way to keep the way to the tree of life".

Now it is very interesting to notice that the cherubims returned and you have their return in Hebrews 9:5 "And over it the cherubims of glory shadowing the mercyseat".

Their sword has changed to their shadow, but there is something more. Upon the veil of that great and wonderful separation barrier cherubims were embroidered. You can find that over in the book of Exodus. Turn to Exodus 26:31 "And thou shalt make a vail of blue," I want you to remember this, we will come back to it, "and purple, and scarlet and fine twined linen of cunning work; with cherubims shall it be made'.

So on this great veil were these great living creatures, the cherubim, who guarded the way to the tree of life and they in type guarded the way to the mercy seat as well as overshadowing it.

Now, who drew aside this veil once a year? It was a man of the tribe of Levi and only a man of the tribe of Levi. No other person had any right to the priesthood, but the Lord Jesus Christ. He was not of the tribe of Levi. He had no right to the priesthood, so He had not, under the Jewish economy, the right to go and part the veil. Who was responsible for that great veil to be there? That veil was there by the command of God to block the way because of the sins of the world of sinners, a human hand could draw it aside just for a moment and enter and sprinkle the blood and return. That was a very temporary opening and it was only for one man of a particular tribe. But what do we read? We read that this veil was rent from the top to the bottom. It was not partially rent. It did not decay and fall into tatters. This veil was rent, starting from the top to the bottom. Now that veil was so constructed that no human energy could tear it. It was thick, it was folded. We have already read to you there was purple cloth in it, there was scarlet cloth in it, there was fine twined linen upon it and it was heavily embroidered. No human power could rend this veil. Of course, if man had been tearing it he would have torn it from the bottom to the top, the top being well beyond his reach when he would be standing on the ground in the temple.

THE RENDING OF THE VEIL

It was the power of the voice of Christ in His final loud cry that rent that veil. "It is finished". When Christ said that, the temple was finished; the Mosaic ceremony was finished; the veil was unnecessary and no more needed. The priesthood was no more, the need to shed the blood of animals was no more, for God's Word from the mouth of the Saviour rent the veil.

Could I say, there is no question, in all the history of the Jews, that this did not happen. If you read all the antiquities of Josephus, if you read all the histories written by unbelieving Jews they never, in all history, question what is written in the Gospel because it was something that was the talk of the hour. Can't you imagine the conversation between two Jews meeting in a street of Jerusalem, "Did you hear when that man of Galilee died on that cross and expired, the veil of the temple, our temple, was split in two from the top to the bottom." This rending of the veil has never been challenged by any historian of Israel or any unbeliever of the Jewish race. It happened. The old economy had passed and had passed forever.

The hand of the priest pulled back the veil once a year to let him in but he did not let God out. God remained behind in the mercy seat, but when the veil was rent by the Saviour it was a two-way street. God came out to pardon His people in mercy and to bring them in to the Father's house in grace. That is the message of this parted veil. God with us, Emmanuel. He is no longer behind the veil. He no longer rests at the mercy seat but, praise God, He is Emmanuel, God with us. He has rent the veil in twain.

WHAT WAS THE REAL VEIL?

But this of course is a type.

What was the real veil? The real veil was the flesh of the Lord Jesus. If you turn over to the book of Hebrews chapter 10:19, It says "Having therefore boldness to enter into the holiest," you don't need to worry, you can be bold to enter in. You don't need to hang your head and try to sneak in, there is no sneaking-in needed. The barricade is away, completely removed, so you walk in with boldness to the throne of grace. "By a new and living way." What is that way? The blood of Jesus. How did He consecrate that way? By the veil, that is to say His flesh. His flesh was the veil. That is most interesting. His flesh, His body, His humanity, was that veil.

You know, if you turn in your Testament to Matthew's Gospel 27, you will find something preceded the rending of that veil. You will find there the story of the cross. You will find there the story of those who parted His garments. Verse 34 "They gave him vinegar to drink mingled with gall; and when he had tasted thereof, he would not drink. And they crucified him, and parted his garments, casting lots; that it might be fulfilled which was spoken by the prophet, They parted my garments among them and upon my vesture did they cast lots." Then if you go on through the reading you will find that there was one garment they did not part and that was His robe. They did not tear it asunder. What was that robe? It was the robe that covered the body of Christ as He walked on this earth. Behind that robe was the sinless humanity of the Son of God, and no man could tear one rent in the covering of the sinless body of the Son of God, but on the cross the veil was rent from top to bottom.

Last night, as I was studying this text I discovered that the first blows that fell on Christ in punishment were blows upon His head. Rending the veil, the flesh, from the top to the bottom. Before they spiked His feet they had already crowned His head with thorns. Before they spiked His feet they had already torn the hairs from off His face. Before they spiked His feet they had already beaten Him on the head and spat upon Him. The veil rent from the top to the bottom! It is in the rending of that veil that we have a way into the Holiest of all.

I remember years ago hearing a young man singing in our old church these words -

Once our blessed Christ of beauty
Was veiled off from human view,
But through suffering, death and sorrow,
He has rent the veil in two.

Yes, He is with God the Father,
Interceding there for you,
For He is the mighty conqueror,
Since He rent the veil in two.

Holy angels bow before Him,
Men of earth give praises due.
For He is the Well Beloved,
Since He rent the veil in two.

Throughout time and endless ages,
Heights and depths of love so true,
He alone can be the giver,
Since He rent the veil in two.

Oh behold the Man of Sorrows,
Oh behold Him in full view.
Lo! He is the Mighty Conqueror,
Since He rent the veil in two.

AMEN AND AMEN!

The FIFTH VEIL Christ rent at Calvary
the veil of the rocks and earth

PART ONE

SCRIPTURE READING LUKE ~ 19: 28-48

"And when He thus has spoken, he went before, ascending up to Jerusalem. And it came to pass, when he was come nigh to Bethphage and Bethany, at the mount called the mount of Olives, he sent two of his disciples. Saying, Go ye into the village over against you; in the which at your entering ye shall find a colt tied, whereon yet never man sat: loose him, and bring him hither. And if any man ask you, Why do ye loose him? thus shall ye say unto him, Because the Lord hath need of him. And they that were sent went their way, and found even as he had said unto them. And as they were loosing the colt, the owners thereof said unto them, Why loose ye the colt? And they said, The Lord hath need of him. And they brought him to Jesus: and they cast their garments upon the colt, and they set Jesus thereon. And as he went, they spread their clothes in the way. And when he was come nigh, even now at the descent of the mount of Olives, the whole multitude of the disciples began to rejoice and praise God with a loud voice for all the mighty works that they had seen; Saying, Blessed be the King that cometh in the name of the Lord: peace in heaven, and glory in the highest. And some of the Pharisees from among the multitude said unto him, Master, rebuke thy disciple. And he answered and said unto them, I tell you that, if these should hold their peace,

the stones would immediately cry out. And when he was come near, he beheld the city, and wept over it, Saying, If thou hadst known, even thou, at least in this thy day, the things which belong unto thy peace! but now they are hid from thine eyes. For the days shall come upon thee, that thine enemies shall cast a trench about thee, and compass thee round, and keep thee in on every side. And shall lay thee even with the ground, and thy children within thee; and they shall not leave in thee one stone upon another; because thou knewest not the time of thy visitation. And he went into the temple, and began to cast out them that sold therein, and them that bought; Saying unto them, It is written, My house is the house of prayer but ye have made it a den of thieves. And he taught daily in the temple. But the chief priests and scribes and the chief of the people sought to destroy him. And could not find what they might do: for all the people were very attentive to hear him."

One of the greatest themes in the Bible is the theme of Calvary's cross and the atonement which was made for sinners by Christ through His sufferings on the accursed tree. We have been looking at the veils which were rent at Calvary.

We have noticed already the veil of darkness which Jesus rent at the cross, and the veil of separation which He rent at the cross. We have noticed the veil of death which He rent at the cross, and have noticed the veil of the temple which He also rent.

We now come to the veil of the earth and the rocks.

Turn with me to Matthew's Gospel 27:51 and read this sentence "And, behold, the veil of the temple was rent in twain from the top to the bottom; and the earth did quake, and the rocks rent." That last clause of this text - "and the earth did quake, and the rocks rent". Any study of the four Gospels - Matthew, Mark, Luke and John can only be profitable and edifying if we keep in mind the objective of the Holy Spirit when He inspired Matthew, Mark, Luke and John to pen these Gospels.

THE PORTRAITS OF CHRIST IN THE GOSPEL

Each Gospel is a portrait of our Lord Jesus Christ but each Gospel is different, because each Gospel brings out a certain office which Jesus Christ held and a certain fulfilment of that office or character as He walked Incarnate among the sons of men.

Now this fourfold Gospel, given to us in Matthew, Mark, Luke and John is spoken of in direct prophecy in the Old Testament. It is also revealed in the picturesque types of the Old Testament. Let me illustrate it briefly to you. In the Old Testament Christ was given the peculiar title of The Branch.

Turn with me to Jeremiah 23:5, you will read there "Behold the days come saith the Lord that I will raise unto David a righteous Branch and a King." So this Branch in Jeremiah is characterised as being Christ, the King.

CHRIST THE SOVEREIGN IN MATTHEW

Those words, Christ the King, fit the Gospel of Matthew as your glove would fit your hand, because Matthew's Gospel is the Gospel of Christ the King. All its references and all its emphasis is upon the Kingly character of Christ. What is the question in the second chapter? Where is He that is born King?

So Matthew's Gospel is the Gospel of Christ the Sovereign, the King. You will never understand it until you view Him in His Kingly capacity. That is why interpreters of Matthew have missed their way and put false interpretations on Matthew's Gospel, because they did not realise that the one supreme emphasis of Matthew's Gospel is Christ the Sovereign King.

CHRIST THE SERVANT IN MARK

Turn to Mark's Gospel, how different it is. Matthew starts with the lineage. Of course a king has got to have a lineage, a genealogy. Every member of that past long list is important to the standing of the King. A servant does not need any lineage. No one cares who his parents were or who his forefathers or ancestors were, so Mark starts with Christ without any lineage because Christ is revealed in Mark as the Servant. Again as your glove fits your hand so the picture of Christ the Servant fits so spectacularly and specially in Mark's gospel.

Could I just give you the reference in the Old Testament to Mark's Gospel, Zechariah 3:8. Again this word Branch is used. It is used in that connection. "Hear now, O Joshua the high priest, thou, and thy fellows that sit before thee; for they are men wondered at; for behold, I will bring forth my servant the Branch". The first reference in Jeremiah was the Branch, the King. The second reference is the

Branch, the Servant. Turn over to Zechariah 6:12, you have another reference, "Speak unto him saying, Thus speaketh the Lord of hosts, saying, Behold the man whose name is the Branch."

CHRIST THE SAVIOUR IN LUKE

Luke's Gospel is the Gospel of Christ the Saviour, the Man Christ Jesus, the One who came not to be ministered unto but to minister, and to give His life a ransom for the many.

You say there is a genealogy in Luke's Gospel. Of course there is, but it does not take you back to David the king only or to Abraham, the friend of God. It goes further than Matthew's genealogy. It takes you back to the first man on earth, Adam. Why? Because Luke's Gospel is the Gospel of Christ the Man, the Man of Sorrows and acquainted with grief. The last reference to the Branch, I want to refer you to, is Isaiah 4:2 "In that day shall the branch of the Lord be beautiful and glorious, and the fruit of the earth shall be excellent and comely for them that are escaped of Israel." Notice how this fits the Gospel of John so completely. We read here that in that day shall the Branch of the Lord, notice the word Lord is in capital letters in the Hebrew, that is Jehovah - God. So the Branch is God, is the Lord.

CHRIST THE SON IN JOHN

In John's Gospel it is the Gospel of the Son, the eternal Son of God. It starts off with the words "In the beginning was the word and the word was with God, and the word was God".

So there are four Branches in prophecy. One of a Sovereign, one of a Servant, one of a Saviour and one of a Son. They were prophesies of the fourfold Gospel of our Lord Jesus Christ.

But as I said this morning, we not only have this four-foldedness of the Gospel in prophesy in the Old Testament but we have it in type in the Old Testament. Turn over to the book of Exodus 26. Last week we were dealing with this veil, Exodus 26:31 "Thou shalt make a veil" of what? Four materials, "blue, purple, scarlet and fine twined linen of cunning work" and then notice this "with cherubim, the angels."

In cunning work upon it shall it be made. Four materials, those four materials speak to us of the four Gospels. Matthew is the Gospel of Blue, the heavenly King. Mark is the Gospel of purple, a royal King who has become a Servant. "He who was rich yet for our sakes became poor that we, through His poverty might be rich." Scarlet, you remember they took His robe off Him and they dressed Him in scarlet because He was to be the Saviour of the world. The Gospel of Luke is the scarlet. The fine twined linen speaks to us of the purity of Christ and His purity speaks of His Deity.

But notice that this veil was hung upon four pillars. That is what the Gospel is. These four Gospels are the pillars on which hang these fourfold portraits of Christ. How were these pillars made? They were made of the hard wood of the desert, the little bush of the desert, the bush that Moses saw one day burning and not consumed. What does that speak of? That speaks of the flesh, the body. Christ is bone of our bone and flesh of our flesh. He took not upon Him the nature of angels but of the seed of Abraham.

THE LINK WITH THE CHERUBIM

So in these Gospels we have revealed the Godman, the Man Christ Jesus. But look, it is linked with the cherubim. Why this link with the cherubim? Turn over to Revelation 4:7 and you will find the description of the cherubim "The first beast," (these were the cherubim) "was like a lion, and the second beast was like a calf, and the third beast had a face as a man, and the fourth beast was like a flying eagle". Please notice three from earth and one from heaven. The lion is the king of beasts. Matthew is the Gospel of the King. The calf is the animal to serve, the oxen. Mark is the Gospel of the Servant. The third is the face of the man because Christ in Luke is the Man. Those are things of earth. But John's Gospel takes us into the heavens, it takes us to the flying eagle, that creature which rises further than any other creature into the heights and Jesus Christ, of course, is the Creator who came from the heights to this world.

When you are reading the Scriptures you should mark the four-foldedness of certain texts. I throw out a challenge to you today that every text in the Old Testament which has a four-fold prophesy on Christ and every Scripture in the New Testament which has a fourfold statement of Christ, they all coincide absolutely with Matthew, Mark, Luke and John.

THE FOUR-FOLDEDNESS

The other day I was reading my Bible and I was looking in the first chapter of Corinthians. I read there this verse "But of him are ye in Christ Jesus who is made unto us ..." When I saw that I said I am going to get something interesting here. He was made unto us wisdom. There is the wisdom of the King. He was made unto us righteousness, there is the righteousness of the Servant, for Christ lived for us to make us a righteousness that could be imputed to us.

"Upon a life I did not live, upon a death I did not die, Another's life, another's death, I stake my all eternally."

He is made unto us wisdom, that is Matthew. He is made unto us sanctification. What is sanctification? Sanctification is separation, and Christ was the separated Man. Holy, Harmless, Undefiled, Separate from sinners, the Flawless, Harmless, Crimeless, Sinless, Spotless, Son of God. That is Luke. But redemption, Jehovah Tsidkenu, the Lord our righteousness, who has become the Lord, our Redeemer. So look for the fours both in prophecy and in promise and in precept.

THE BEGINNINGS AND ENDS OF THE GOSPELS

When you say to me "Preacher, you have had a very long introduction today." Yes, because we are going to interpret this Scripture right we have got to get our context right. I would have you to notice the beginnings and endings of the Gospels. I might just make a little commercial here. We have a tape which is still available, on the beginnings and endings of the Gospels showing that they dovetail completely.

In Matthew's Gospel in the first chapter you will find a man called Joseph and in the last chapter of Matthew you will find a man called Joseph. The two Josephs of Matthew will tell you a wonderful story.

Mark commences with the start of the Gospel and the last verse of Mark is the spread of the Gospel.

Luke begins in the temple with old priest Zechariah and ends in the temple. Just have a look at it for yourself.

In the first chapter of John you have Christ speaking for the first time to John the disciple and to Simon Peter and in the last chapter of John you have Christ speaking for the last time to John and Simon Peter. So just look at the start and the finish of each of the Gospels.

A man said to me one day "What proof have you of the ascension of Christ to heaven?" I said, "All the Gospels tell me that Christ went to heaven." He said "Do they?" He set me down and I had to hang my head in shame because all the Gospels do not talk about the ascension of Christ. Just go home and read them. Some of you are looking at me as if I have taken leave of my senses but I have not.

There is a reason for that. Some of the Gospels do not tell you of Christ's ascension. You will find when you read the Gospels and the emphasis they are making.

Now having said that, could I say everything in Matthew's Gospel has to be related to the Kingship of Christ. Everything in Mark's Gospel has to be related to the Service of Christ. Everything in Luke's Gospel has to be related to the Manhood of Christ and everything in John's Gospel to the Godhead of Christ.

THE RELATIONS OF THE GOSPELS

Now we turn to Matthew's Gospel and could I say something to you as well. There are some things that are said in all the Gospels and are recorded.

What you need to do is to go home and get a notebook and put down Matthew, Mark, Luke and John and when reading those books make a note of what is in them and you will find that there are some things in every Gospel that are common to them all.

Then there are some things which are only in three of the Gospels and they are not in the fourth, and there are some things that are in only two Gospels and not in the other two.

Also, there are some things only in one of the Gospels.

You will never understand that except you take this key that I am giving you. Christ the Sovereign. Christ the Servant. Christ the Saviour and Christ the Son. If you get that you will not see through a glass darkly, you will see face to face and recognise the Sovereign, Servant, Son and Saviour.

Now isn't it peculiar that none of the other Gospels have anything whatsoever to say to us about the rending of the rocks and the great earthquake of Calvary.

MATTHEW ALONE RECORDS THIS RENDING

If you turn over to 27:51, my text (I am just getting to my text now) "And the earth did quake and the rocks rent." Go home and read Mark and Luke and John, there is not a word of it. Why is that? I will tell you. The word that is used here is the word "earth". It is in the Greek text and it deals with the land mass, in distinction from the sea which is the water mass, or the sky which is the air mass. Here we have the whole land mass shaken. Writers talk about a day when the whole earth had a colossal earthquake. It is only written in Matthew's Gospel. The other Gospels do not mention it. Is that not strange? The rocks were torn asunder. Other Gospels do not mention it. Did Matthew make it up? No he did not make it up at all. I would not care if there was no confirmation from writers at the time. That would not worry me because God's Word says it and I believe God's Word. That is the testimony on which we stand. Why was that? Because it was the eternal majesty, the King of kings and the King of the whole earth who died at Calvary. Was it any wonder that the whole earth shook. Was it any wonder that the great rocks were smashed!

Father bless your Holy Word to our hearts and do us good as we worship Christ the Sovereign, Christ the Servant, Christ the Saviour and Christ the Son, who loved me and gave Himself for me.

AMEN AND AMEN

The FIFTH VEIL Christ rent at Calvary
the veil of the rocks and earth

PART TWO

SCRIPTURE READING ~ HEBREWS 12:18-28

*"For ye are not come unto the mount that might be touched, and
that burned with fire, nor unto blackness, and darkness, and
tempest, And the sound of a trumpet, and the voice of words; which
voice they that heard entreated that the word should not be spoken
to them any more: (For they could not endure that which was
commanded, And if so much as a beast touch the mountain, it shall
be stoned, or thrust through with a dart: And so terrible was the sight,
that Moses said, I exceedingly fear and quake:) But ye are come
unto mount Sion, and unto the city of the living God, the heavenly
Jerusalem, and to an innumerable company of angels, to the
general assembly and church of the firstborn, which are written in
heaven, and to God the Judge of all, and to the spirits of just men
made perfect, And to Jesus the mediator of the new covenant, and to
the blood of sprinkling, that speaketh better things than that of Abel.
See that ye refuse not him that speaketh. For if they escaped not who
refused him that spake on earth, much more shall not we escape, if
we turn away from him that speaketh from heaven: Whose voice
then shook the earth: but now he hath promised, saying, Yet once
more I shake not the earth only, but also heaven. And this word, Yet
once more, signifieth the removing of those things that are shaken,*

as of things that are made, that those things which cannot be shaken may remain. Wherefore we receiving a kingdom which cannot be moved, let us have grace, whereby we may serve God acceptably with reverence and godly fear: For our God is a consuming fire."

Turn with me to Matthew's Gospel 27:51 "And behold the veil of the temple was rent in twain from the top to the bottom and the earth did quake and the rocks rent." I introduced this subject last Lord's Day, and could I say cassette tapes of all these messages are available from our recording studio which you will find under the second gallery there.

We dealt with the setting of the Gospels - Matthew, Mark, Luke and John and I pointed out that those things only mentioned in one of the Gospels can only be understood when we discover the peculiarity of that Gospel. Matthew's peculiarity is that it is the Gospel of the King. Mark's Gospel is the Gospel of the Servant. Luke's Gospel is the Gospel of the Saviour and John's Gospel is the Gospel of God manifest in flesh.

So Matthew is the Gospel of the Sovereign, Mark is the Gospel of the Servant. Luke is the Gospel of the Saviour and John is the Gospel of the Son.

PECULIAR TO MATTHEW'S GOSPEL

Now this incident about Calvary is not recorded in Mark's Gospel. It is not recorded in Luke's Gospel. It is not recorded in John's Gospel. It is only recorded in the Gospel of Matthew, because it highlights that the One who died upon the cross was Christ the King of kings and Lord of lords and no wonder the death of the King of the whole earth caused the whole earth to quake and the rocks to be rent.

The timing of this world-wide quaking of the earth and the rending of the rocks is to be noted. You will notice that this text commences with the word "behold". That word means look and see. It calls for inspection and meditation and consideration and careful scrutiny. The quaking of the earth and the rending of the rocks was a response and testimony to the power of the King.

Turn with me to Luke 19. There the Lord Jesus Christ is about to enter the city of Jerusalem. A great crowd gathers as He descends from the Mount of Olives. Luke's Gospel 19:37 "And when he was come nigh, even now at the descent of the mount of Olives, the whole multitude of the disciples began to rejoice and praise God with a loud voice for all the mighty works that they had seen; Saying, Blessed be the King" note the words "that cometh in the name of the Lord: peace in heaven and glory in the highest." That was the song of the angels at His birth. "Glory to God in the highest and on earth, peace, goodwill towards men." Where that is used you will remember wise men said "Where is he that is born?" what? "King!" Notice the emphasis on His Kingship. "And some of the Pharisees from among the multitude said unto him, Master, rebuke thy disciples, And he answered and said unto them, I tell you that, if these should hold their peace, the stones would immediately cry out." At the death of Christ the stones immediately cried out. What a cry it was. It shook the whole earth.

WHEN THE STONES CRIED OUT

When the King was passing by Jesus said "If they stopped their singing and their shouting and their praises the stones would cry out." As the King passed into the darkness of death to descend into the place where the souls of Old Testament saints were in captivity to lead captives and to give gifts unto men the King cried out.

Those standing around were stunned with a mighty fear. A great fear fell upon the very hardened soldiers, if you look with me at verse 54 "Now the centurion and they that were with him watching Jesus saw the earth quake and these things that were done they feared greatly." This earthquake was no trifle. This was the testimony of the earth that Christ, the mighty Maker died, for man, the creature's, sin.

The first blood of man shed on earth was shed in Genesis chapter four. Something happened in Genesis chapter four. The earth co-operated with Cain in a massive cover up. It received the blood of the first man to die on earth. The record says that God had something to say to Cain about that blood.

EARTH AND SHED BLOOD

Turn over with me to Genesis chapter four. This is of vital importance. Verse ten of chapter four "What hast thou done? the voice of thy brother's blood crieth unto me from the ground. And now art thou cursed from the earth, which has opened her mouth to receive thy brother's blood from thy hand." The first of man's blood was covered over by the earth, but when this happened, the blood that was shed by Christ from His heart had not yet been poured out upon the earth.

So here we have the cry of the earth, not in a cover-up of the blood, but the cry of the earth in a testimony to the fact that there was no blood ever shed like this or no death was ever like this, and the Godman who died on the cross is the special Man, the only Man like Him, and there was never blood like it before and there will never be blood like it again.

THE RESPONSIVE TESTIMONY

The rending, shall I repeat, was a responsive testimony to the power of the King. It was also a universal testimony to the reign of the King. The word that is used for earth here is the "land mass" as opposed to the mass of the earth which is covered with water, and opposed to that part of creation which is filled with air. All the whole continents of the world, the entire world, shook.

That is not going to happen again until the eternal age when God shall shake this old planet of ours and it will be rolled away and purged with everlasting fire. But the earth shook, the whole earth. Heathen writers across the then-known world recorded that at that time there was a strange phenomenon, the whole earth shook. When Samson died he took the pillars of the temple and he shook them. When Jesus died upon the cross this earth, of its own accord, shook.

There have been earthquakes occurring through natural causes, but this earthquake had a supernatural cause.

"Well may the sun in darkness hide,
And shut her glories in,
When God the mighty Maker died,
For man, the creature's, sin"

The sun was millions of miles away, but the very place where the cross was erected, the very place where the body of Jesus Christ hung in awful suffering and shame for the sins of you and me, that earth was going to shake as a testimony, a universal testimony, to the reign of the King.

This was no regular earthquake caused by natural processes. This was an earthquake whose timing demonstrates its supernatural divinity. After the loud cry "It is finished" and the whispered words "Into thy hand I commend my spirit", what happened? The veil of the temple was torn from top to bottom by the Divine Hand of God. "The earth did quake and the rocks rent."

THE THREE GREAT HAPPENINGS

We will be looking at the rending of the graves. Listen to it, "and the graves were opened". Three great happenings. Bishop Nicholson, who wrote a very fine study on the cross, entitled the Miracles of Calvary, says there are four coincidences here which should be carefully marked. 1, It coincided with the death of the Lord Jesus. 2, It coincided with the miraculous rending of the graves 3, It coincided with the rending of the temple, and, 4, It coincided with the cry of victory "It is finished".While everything else shook the cross did not shake. It was the unshakable cross. In that shaking the cross stood eternally firm.

> The cross it standeth fast, Hallelujah!
> Defying every blast, Hallelujah!
> The winds of hell have blown,
> The world its hate has shown,.
> Yet it is not o'erthrown,
> Hallelujah for the cross!

That is the message of this earthquake. While the earth can shake, the cross shall never be shaken. When I talk to you about the cross I am not talking about the wood of the cross, I am talking about the work done on the cross for sinners. It stands forever. When this old planet is no more and there is a new heaven and a new earth in which dwelleth righteousness, and the eternal ages after the millennium reign of Christ are ushered in, the cross will still be the centre of the glory and the centre of the songs of the saints. We will be singing about the cross for all eternity. The cross is the greatest thing God ever did or ever could do. The cross exhausted the Omnipotence of God and His Omniscience.

THE CROSS, THE HIGHEST SUMMIT

At the cross, the highest summit that the feet of Deity would ever stand on, was stood upon.

The cross is the highest revelation of the heart of God for sinners, and the love that flows in His heart for poor, lost, guilty sinners. Thank God for Calvary. No wonder the devil hates it. No wonder the modernists attack it. No wonder it is the scorn of unbelieving scholarship today. But thank God, we believe in the cross, we have been saved by this cross, we have been kept by this cross. By this cross we have a key that opens the golden gates of the eternal city, and by this cross we shall approach the very throne of God and stand unashamed in robes washed in the Saviour's blood, to be part of the family of God for ever and ever.

The rending of the rocks was a universal testimony to the reign of the King. The rending of the rocks was the final testimony to the rending of another mountain, the mountain of the law, Mount Sinai. We were reading about it there in the twelfth chapter of Hebrews. You can go home and read about that mountain. When God descended upon Sinai there was an earthquake. It was not the earthquake of atonement, it was the earthquake of judgment. It was the earthquake of God's wrath, and there was the sound of a trumpet and the voice of words. The whole camp of Israel shook and Israel said "Let God speak no more to us. We cannot listen to the dreadful words of God." While Sinai spoke of the depths of sin, Calvary speaks of the depths of love. While Sinai spoke of ruin, Calvary speaks of regeneration.

ABSORBING SINAI

It was Bishop Nicholson who said Calvary absorbed the fiery Sinai.

"By the darkness which drank up the light of day and caused men's hearts to fail them for fear, and by that wail of suffering ringing through the darkened heavens whose depths of anguish none but He had ever uttered, it became manifest even to the senses of men that Calvary was more awful and far more powerful than Sinai because Calvary swallowed all the fire of Sinai forever."

The testimony of Sinai was a broken law given whole into the hands of Moses, and before he got it to the camp he smashed it on the ground. But Calvary speaks to me of a law that was kept - the Sinless, Spotless, Flawless, Crimeless, Harmless, Son of God, kept that law, for He was the ark which kept safe the law of God. What did He offer on the cross? He offered His perfect life.

As He lived He kept God's law perfectly. He dotted every "i" and stroked every "t" and after the ending of 30 years walk on this earth, heaven opened and God testified. What did God say? "This is my beloved Son in whom I am well pleased" So Calvary swallowed Sinai and its awful curse. That terrible mountain of ruin and reprobation was swallowed by a mountain of redemption and regeneration. That is what the rending of the rocks meant. That is what the great universal earthquake meant.

ANTICIPATION OF FULL LIBERATION

This rending was the anticipation of the testimony of this earth's full liberation from the curse of the law. Turn over to Romans chapter eight. If you read it carefully you will find there are three groanings in this chapter. There is the groaning of the saints. There is the groaning of the Spirit. There is also the groaning of this old earth. Verse 18 "For I reckon that the sufferings of this present time are not worthy to be compared to the glory that shall be revealed in us. For the earnest expectation of the creature waiteth for the manifestation of the sons of God. For the creature was made subject to vanity, not willingly, but by reason of him who has subjected the same in hope because the creature itself also shall be delivered from the bondage of corruption into the glorious liberty of the children of God. For we know that the whole creation groaneth and travaileth in pain together until now."

What was this earthquake? It was the first groan of creation based upon Christ's death which anticipated the manifestation of the sons of God, and the manifestation of the sons of God would come about when Jesus would return to this earth. So the first groan came from this earth which would be liberated in the great millennial day of Christ's kingdom on earth.

THE ETERNAL SUNRISE

There will be sunrise in the eternal world, and no other sunrise could ever be likened to them because ours is a sin-cursed world. There will be sunsets of deeper beauty in the eternal age than we ever witnessed in our age because our age is cursed by time.

The whole creation suffers from the curse of the law, but praise be to our Lord, here is the first groan of this earth when He dies and it anticipates the full liberation of this world of ours.

What a day that is going to be!

There is a verse which says:

"Sunshine such as earth has never known.
Sunrise such as earth has never known,
Shall fill these skies with mirth and smiles and beauty.
Erasing each sad wrinkle from their brow.
It is a long curse deeply graven there.
The whole creation groans and waits to hear Christ's voice.
That shall restore her comeliness and make her rejoice.
Come Lord and wipe away the curse, the sin, the stain,
And make this blighted world of ours, our own fair world again,
Come then Lord Jesus come."

When He comes the earth will give its final groan and be liberated into the glorious liberty of the children of God. What a cross! What a conflict was there fought. What a conquest was there gained. We say with Bunyan's Pilgrim "Blessed cross, blessed sepulchre, blessed rather be the Man that there was put to shame for me".

May we love Him with all our hearts. May we give our lives afresh to Him and may we be among those that are numbered as the sons of God.

For Jesus Sake.

AMEN AND AMEN!

The SIXTH VEIL Christ rent at Calvary
the veil of the graves

SCRIPTURE READING ~ II CORINTHIANS 5

"For we know that if our earthly house of this tabernacle were dissolved, we have a building of God, an house not made with hands, eternal in the heavens. For in this we groan, earnestly desiring to be clothed upon with our house which is from heaven: If so be that being clothed we shall not be found naked. For we that are in this tabernacle do groan, being burdened: not for that we would be unclothed, but clothed upon, that mortality might be swallowed up of life. Now he that hath wrought us for the selfsame thing is God, who also hath given unto us the earnest of the Spirit. Therefore we are always confident, knowing that while we are at home in the body, we are absent from the Lord: (For we walk by faith, not by sight:) We are confident, I say, and willing rather to be absent from the body, and to be present with the Lord. Wherefore we labour, that, whether present or absent, we may be accepted of him. For we must all appear before the judgment seat of Christ; that every one may receive the things done in his body, according to that he hath done, whether it be good or bad, Knowing therefore the terror of the Lord, we persuade men; but we are made manifest unto God; and I trust also are made manifest in your consciences. For we commend not ourselves again unto you, but give you occasion to glory on our behalf,

*that ye may have somewhat to answer them which glory in appear-
ance, and not in heart. For whether we be beside ourselves, it is to
God: or whether we be sober, it is for your cause. For the love of
Christ constraineth us; because we thus judge, that if one died for
all, then were all dead: And that he died for all, that they which live
should not henceforth live unto themselves, but unto him which died
for them, and rose again. Wherefore henceforth know we no man
after the flesh: yea, though we have known Christ after the flesh, yet
now henceforth know we him no more. Therefore if any man be in
Christ, he is a new creature: old things are passed away; behold, all
things are become new. And all things are of God, who hath reconciled us to himself by Jesus Christ, and hath given to us the ministry
of reconciliation. To wit, that God was in Christ, reconciling the world
unto himself, not imputing their trespasses unto them; and hath committed unto us the word of reconciliation. Now then we are ambas-
sadors for Christ, as though God did beseech you by us: we pray you
in Christ's stead, be ye reconciled to God. For he hath made him to
be sin for us, who knew no sin; that we might be made the righteousness of God in him."*

We have looked at the rending of the veil of darkness. We have looked at
the rending of the veil of separation. We have looked at the rending of the veil of
death. We have looked at the rending of the veil of the temple and we have looked
at the rending of the earth and the rocks in the mighty earthquake.

Now we turn, in our Bibles, to Matthew 27:52-53, "And the graves were
opened; and many bodies of the saints which slept arose, And came out of the
graves after his resurrection, and went into the holy city, and appeared unto many".
The rending of the veil of the graves.

THE GRAVEYARD AT THE CROSS

Around the cross of Christ was a graveyard. In fact, the hill Golgotha means
the skull hill, the place of a skull. In answer to our Lord's loud cry of "Finished"
something happened. Number one, the veil of the temple was rent in twain.
Number two, the veil of the earth and the rocks was shaken and rent by a mighty
earthquake. Number three, the tombs, the graves, the sepulchres around the
cross were broken open and the bodies buried there were exposed.

I want you to notice some vital things about this great supernatural act. I want you to notice the predestination of the split second of God's timing.

THE PREDESTINATION OF THE TIMING

God works on a split-second time table, if we can use a time-warp word with the activities of the eternal God. But the eternal God is also the God of all time.

It was God Who created time and God, one day, will uncreate time. It was God Who made the clock of time and wound it up. It will be God's intervention that will cause the clock of time to cease its ticking for evermore. Time will not stop a minute too late or a minute too soon. It will stop on the split-second of God's predetermination or predestination.

It started when God commanded it. One day God will command forever the cessation of time.

The face of this earth was shattered by the cry of Christ. The great rocks were rent and the graves were opened and the bodies that lay in those graves were exposed. The force of the authority of Christ's word is seen in the rending of the earth and the rending of the rocks, but the design behind that force is seen in the opening of the graves.

These graves were rocky sepulchres, caves, some of them chiselled by man and some of them natural excavations. When a corpse was buried in these tombs a great stone sealed the entrance to the death cavern. But when Jesus Christ shouted "Finished," the doors of the tomb were shattered and broken and there lay exposed to all who passed by the dead bodies of those that were buried there.

THE PREDETERMINATION OF THE GRAVES

While we want to consider the predestination of the split-second timing of God, we need also to dwell for a moment at the predetermination of the graves themselves. It is interesting to note while Joseph of Arimathaea was planning a tomb for the dead body of Christ, a tomb that would be sealed by the great stone rolled up and into its entrance, that God, on the other hand, through the power of Christ's work was not preparing a tomb or sealing it, He was breaking open the tombs and unsealing them.

You will remember also that at the tomb of Christ the state and the church united to further seal that tomb. Jewry and Caesar's empire joined in unison to seal the cave's door, the great rocky stone. Further, the soldiers of Rome stood outside to guard that tomb so that none might break the seal or roll away the stone or shatter the place where the body of Christ was laid. What stupid fools they were! What stupid fools the soldiers of the Emperor were! What stupid fools the great powers of the state of Rome were! Who could stop the Almighty Christ rising from the dead? Did He not say "I have power?" There are two words in the Greek text commonly used for power. One is *exousia* which means authority. The other is *dunamis* which means actual force. *Dunamis* is the word from which we get dynamite. It is actual force. But the word that is used by Christ is the other word, authority. "I have the authority to lay down my life. I have the authority to take it again. This commandment have I received of my Father". Think of that for a moment. Christ has the authority to dismiss His person from the human body. But He had also the authority to donate His person back into that body and bring it forth in resurrection life.

Those graves, supernaturally shattered and opened, were limited in number. All the graves in the burying place around the tomb were not opened. Look with me please at verse 52 "And the graves were opened and many bodies of the saints which slept arose and came out of the graves." Around that graveyard there were scores of graves that held the bodies of unpardoned, unforgiven sinners. But among them there were graves that held the remains of pardoned sinners. Not one grave of an unbelieving soul was disturbed that day. Not one grave or rocky tomb was shattered if in it was the body of an unbeliever. They remained untouched. But predetermination of the graves themselves was manifested in the fact that every one of the believer's graves were shattered and their bodies exposed.

MICROCOSM

This is a microcosm of what is going to happen when Jesus comes. When Jesus comes there is going to be the resurrection of the just. If my dead bones are lying beside the bones of some unbeliever, those bones of that unbeliever will remain untouched and unshaken while my bones will rise and a new body will be prepared to receive my spirit. That will happen to all believers.

What a day that will be when the trumpet will sound and the dead in Christ shall rise first!

The old Puritan was right when he said Christ limited the number of the dead who awake to life. He said, notice please, that when Christ went into the graveyard at Bethany He only stood before one grave and He only commanded that one stone be removed. When He spoke He did not say come forth, if he had said that, everybody in the graveyard would have arisen. He said, "Lazarus, come forth." Some day the Master will call you by your name. When Jesus comes He will name the roll call of His saints and their bodies shall rise again. That is the message that is here told to us in microcosm in this text.

Well may we inquire, whose where these graves which were opened? Who were these saints that after Christ's resurrection left the graves forever? Notice verse 53 "And came out of the graves after his resurrection, and went into the holy city, and appeared unto many". Christ was the firstfruits, but these were sample fruits He plucked up to take with Him on the way to heaven.

DEAD BODIES EXPOSED

The opening of these graves, the rending of the sepulchres, was the first great act. The walls of death's empire were struck such a blow that actually the gates and entrances to those many graves in that hill of graves were rent and the inside of those dark vaults were exposed to the light of the sun.

Those bodies which were seen were passed by by many people, because the place of the skull was close to the city walls. For three days and three nights when anyone passed that hill they saw opened graves and dead bodies. I am sure many a well read Jew in the Scripture, as he passed, thought of that great chapter in Ezekiel which proposed the question, "Can these dead bones live?"

But when John the apostle and Peter ran to Christ's tomb as they passed those graves they did not see one body, because after Christ arose those bodies all arose with Him, every one of them.

If John and Peter had noticed that all the exhumed bodies which were the talk of the whole city were now gone they would have been more prepared to receive the story of the empty tomb and of Christ risen from the dead. Calvary is the place of miracles. The death of Christ is the greatest miracle that God ever wrought and the resurrection of Christ is the greatest seal of that miracle that God could possibly do.

At precisely the time when the Saviour's own door to death, the great stone, was taken away by the hand of an angel, these bodies, exposed, exhibited, an awful gory sight, were suddenly raised from the dead. What does it say? "And many bodies of the saints which slept arose."

The Bible makes it clear that these were the bodies of the saints. As I have already said, around the cross were the graves of both saints and sinners.

THE PRE-INTIMATION OF DEATH'S DESTRUCTION

Could I pass to a third point now, the preintimation of the destruction of death. We sang today a Psalm and could I call your attention to that Psalm, 68. It is a Psalm about the resurrection of our Lord Jesus Christ. You will notice in that Psalm there is something said about that resurrection. Verses 13-20 "Though ye have lien among the pots," that is where those poor bodies lay, in dark Golgotha, the place of the skull. They lay among the pots. "Yet shall ye be as the wings of a dove, covered with silver, and her feathers with yellow gold. When the Almighty scattereth kings in it, it was white as snow in Salmon."

The mighty kings who were shattered at the cross were King Death and King Sin. "The hill of God is as the hill of Bashan; an high hill as the hill of Bashan. Why leap he, ye high hills? this is the hill which God desireth to dwell in; yes, the Lord will dwell in it for ever. The chariots of God are twenty thousand, even thousands of angels: the Lord is among them, as in Sinai, in the holy place. Thou hast ascended on high, thou hast led captivity captive: thou hast received gifts for men; yes, for the rebellious also, that the Lord God might dwell among them. Blessed be the Lord who daily loadeth us with benefits, even the God of our salvation."

It is generally held by Bible expositors that the place of the dead under the Old Testament economy was divided into two places. The place where pardoned souls went after death was called the bosom of Abraham. The place where unpardoned souls went was hell, a place of torments. We don't know much about this but in a few sentences in Luke's Gospel chapter 16 the Lord Jesus Himself lifted the curtain and spoke to us of those two departments of the place of the departed dead before the cross-work was done.

THE WORLD OF THE DEAD

You will remember that He talked about godly Lazarus in the bosom of Abraham, He talked about the rich man tormented in hell, and He talked about a great unpassable chasm, a great gulf between the two. No one could pass over that gulf.

Now, of course, when we die, if we are saved, it is absent from the body and present with the Lord. But when the Old Testament saints died it was absent from the body and present in the bosom of Abraham. Why was that? Why did not the Old Testament saints, pardoned through faith in the same Christ as you and me, (for they looked forward to the cross and we look back), why did they not go immediately to God and to Abraham's bosom? Simply because the price of their redemption was not paid until Jesus Christ died on the cross and His payment was ratified by His resurrection from the tomb. So while they were in the place of comfort and rest they were not yet in the immediate presence of God.

Jesus Christ descended into hades or hell, the place of the departed dead, not to the hell of torments but to the place of the departed dead of pardoned souls. When He came forth He led captivity captive. Those still held under the law and justice of that law were now free because their debts were paid and all the Old Testament saints from Adam to the last saint that died before Jesus rose from the dead were released and they went with Christ to heaven. He led captivity captive and all the Old Testament saints, redeemed spirits, the spirits of just men made perfect, are in the very same place as the redeemed spirits of all those who have died in Christ since the cross to this present day. There is an empty place. There is no one now in Abraham's bosom. They are all with Christ.

RESURRECTION BODIES BEFORE THE GENERAL RESURRECTION

Not all of these saints were resurrected in their bodies, they still await that resurrection, but a special group of them had something else happen. They were given a resurrection body. This is a most interesting subject because there were people who went directly to heaven in the Old Testament. The devil did not like it and he had a fierce controversy about it with Michael the archangel. One of those men was Moses. Moses was buried by God and after God buried Moses He resurrected him. After he was resurrected He took him to heaven and Satan said to Michael "God ought not to have done that, Christ has not yet died, the payment is not yet paid and yet Moses' body is out of the tomb and is now in heaven."

Now Michael was a very wise angel. He did not enter into theological debates with the devil. Do you know what he said? He said, "The Lord rebuke you! Shut up devil. I don't understand what God has done but it is done and Moses is in heaven." Why was Moses taken in a resurrected body to heaven? Because there was a type that had to be practically demonstrated and that type was this, that part of the saints of God of all times will be resurrected from the dead, but not them all.

There was another man whose name was Elijah and he did not die at all. He went up to heaven, not in a chariot of fire but in a whirlwind. Because the chariots of fire remain on earth, they are a type of the presence of God. Elijah went to heaven, what is he a type of? He is a type of those of us who will still be alive when Jesus comes. So there had to be the type in order that the type might be fulfilled. Moses is the type of those of us, if we live till Jesus comes, who will be resurrected and Elijah is the type of those who will be on earth and will be caught up to meet the Lord in the air without death when Jesus comes.

PRE CALVARY DISCUSSION

Those two men appeared on the hill of glory and they talked about the exodus. Now both of them had an exodus. One had an exodus from the tomb and the other had an exodus from the earth directly when they talked with Jesus on the mount of transfiguration. Let me tell you something, the mount of transfiguration is the perfect picture of heaven. You just look at it. People say to me "Will we know one another in heaven?" There was an old Scots woman and her husband was always asking questions of the minister. One day he asked the minister while visiting the house, "Do you think, minister, we will know one another in heaven?" His wife was so exasperated she said "Do you think, John, you will have less sense when you are in heaven than you have now. Don't you know me now?" She was absolutely right.

Peter never saw Moses or Elias but when he was on the mount he recognised them. He said, "Let us build three tabernacles, one for you Lord, one for Moses and one for Elias." I am sure when Peter said that the Lord Jesus laughed, because I want to tell you heaven is not a tabernacle. Heaven is no tent. There is an American song that says, "Build me a cabin in the corner of glory land". The man that wrote that was an idiot and an insulter of the Divine. I am not going to a cabin or a "prefab". I am going to the Father's house of many mansions. There was no tabernacle and the cloud came down. What did they see? Jesus only. Because in the city of God they need no candle nor light of the sun, for the Lord God giveth them light. There is no temple in heaven, for Christ, the Lamb is the Temple thereof.

So we have a perfect picture of the intimation of what is going to happen when our Lord comes. I have a final thought that I will leave with you. We have not only that predemonstration of the resurrection of the saints of all ages but we have the final and glorious intimation of the total destruction of death.

THREE DEATHS

There are three deaths recorded in Scripture that finished in resurrection when the Lord came. Jairus' daughter, the widow of Nain's son and Lazarus. I knew that if I looked at them I would find out something about resurrection.

The first one to be raised was Jairus' daughter. Turn to Matthew 9:24 "He said unto them, Give place: for the maid is not dead, but sleepeth." To us death will only be a sleep. When the people were put forth He went in and took her by the hand. So resurrection came to Jairus' daughter when He took her by the hand. The hand of Christ.

Turn over in your Bible to Luke 7:12 and look at the resurrection of the widow of Nain's son. You will find something different in that resurrection. "There was a dead man carried out, the only son of his mother, and she was a widow: and much people of the city was with her. And when the Lord saw her, he had compassion her, and said unto her, Weep not. And he came and touched the bier." First, He took the daughter of Jairus by the hand, this time He only touched the coffin. The third time, at the tomb of Lazarus, He commanded that the stone be rolled away and He did not touch anything.

There is one thing common to all the resurrections here and that is He spoke. That is common to them all. He spoke to the girl and took her by the hand. He spoke and touched the coffin and He spoke at the grave of Lazarus. All resurrections need one essential and that is the voice of God, the voice of the Son, the Eternal Word.

THE MIGHTY RESURRECTION WORD

That is what the Lord Jesus did at Calvary. He spoke "Finished" and these bodies were exhumed and after the resurrection they arose and went into the holy city. What city is that? Turn to the last chapters of Revelation and you will find the holy city. When I was a boy I used to think that was Jerusalem. Not at all. Those resurrected saints did not walk around Jerusalem like ghosts scaring people. I used to think they simply knocked the door and walked in and said "I am a saint from the Old Testament". No, they appeared in heaven. They showed themselves in heaven resurrected from the dead.

Is not the Bible a wonderful book? Is not God's truth unchangeable and unsearchable and His ways past finding out, for on yonder cross God did the greatest act that God could do. He exhausted His omnipotence, His omniscience and His omnipresence by finding a way to save poor lost sinners and make them the sons of the Eternal for evermore. In that great chapter we read this morning you will notice how the resurrection is linked with the new creation. "If any man be in Christ he is a new creature, old things have passed away and all things have become new."

May every man and woman, boy and girl in this house today be a new creature in Jesus Christ.

AMEN AND AMEN

The SEVENTH VEIL Christ rent at Calvary
the veil of His flesh

PART ONE

SCRIPTURE READING ~ JOHN 19:30-37 & I JOHN 5:6-8

"When Jesus therefore had received the vinegar, he said, It is finished: and he bowed his head, and gave up the ghost. The Jews therefore, because it was the preparation, that the bodies should not remain upon the cross on the sabbath day, (for that sabbath day was an high day,) besought Pilate that their legs might be broken, and that they might be taken away. Then came the soldiers, and brake the legs of the first, and of the other which was crucified with him. But when they came to Jesus, and saw that he was dead already, they brake not his legs: But one of the soldiers with a spear pierced his side, and forthwith came there out blood and water. And he that saw bare record, and his record is true: and he knoweth that he saith true, that ye might believe. For these things were done, that the scripture should be fulfilled, A bone of him shall not be broken. And again another scripture saith, They shall look on him whom they pierced."

"This is he that came by water and blood, even Jesus Christ; not by water only, but by water and blood. And it is the Spirit that beareth witness, because the Spirit is truth. For there are three that bear record in heaven, the Father, the Word, and the Holy Ghost: and these three

are one. And there are three that bear witness in earth, the spirit, and the water, and the blood: and these three agree in one."

We have dealt with Christ's rending of the veil of darkness that covered the cross for a three hour period. We have dealt with the veil of separation which He rent, the separation between Him and the dying thief. As that veil was rent the dying thief was saved. We have looked also at the rending of the veil of death by His conquering of death for ever. We have looked at the veil of the temple that was rent in twain from the top to the bottom, and we have looked at the veil of earth and the rock which were rent after He gave up the ghost. We have looked at the rending of the graves and the resulting resurrections from those graves when Jesus Himself arose from the dead. Today we come to the seventh and the last - the rending of the veil of His flesh.

If you turn over in your New Testament to Hebrews 10:20 "By a new and living way, which he hath consecrated for us, through the veil, that is to say, his flesh". Through the veil, that is to say, His flesh. That great expositor of God's Word, A.W. Pink, in his classic work on the seven cries of Christ from the cross, (a book which every believer should get and study carefully,) states that we should always remember, when we come to study the cross, four things about the death of Christ.

Number one, that His death was **natural**. That is, it was a real death. Jesus Christ really and truly and properly died.

Secondly, it was not only a natural death but it was an **unnatural** death because death had no claim whatsoever upon Him. We die because death has a claim upon us, but Jesus Christ was the sinless, spotless, flawless, crimeless Son of God, so His death was unnatural because death had no claim upon Him.

Thirdly, His death was **preternatural**. What does that mean? It was determined beforehand. Why He should die, when He should die and how He should die.

Last of all, His death was **supernatural** for there never was a death like His. No death of any member of the human race can be compared in any way to the supernatural death of Jesus Christ upon the cross.

Keeping those four things in mind in this passage of Scripture in the Gospel according to John chapter 19: 30-37 you will find three distinct things which underline the whole doing of the cross. You will find first of all, the ratification of Scripture. You will find secondly the identification of the Saviour. You will find thirdly the purification of the sinner.

THE RATIFICATION OF THE SCRIPTURE

Let me deal first of all with the ratification of the Scripture. Look with me at verse 36 and look very carefully, for there is a contrast between these two verses which must be carefully noted. "For these things were done, that the scripture should be fulfilled, A bone of him shall not be broken". Here is a Scripture that must of necessity be fulfilled. It must be fulfilled at this time in the cross work of our Lord Jesus Christ. No bone of His body shall be broken. But then notice "And again another scripture saith." Notice it does not say "another Scripture is fulfilled," for this Scripture is not yet fulfilled, but it emphasises that something must be done at the cross so that in the future this Scripture can be fulfilled.

If this thing is not done, then this Scripture cannot be fulfilled and the Word of God loses its integrity and infallibility. "They shall look on him whom they pierced". Jesus must be pierced. For when He comes again, Israel, according to the prophecy of Zechariah, is going to look on Him whom they pierced. So He must be pierced.

Now when you consider that no bone of His body would be broken, and when you consider that His body would be pierced you will discover that **it seems singularly impossible that these two Scriptures should be fulfilled in their veracity and integrity**. Christ is on the cross. He has died first. Why did He die first? He died first because without His death neither of the dying thieves could have died. Christ is the Lord of life, and death cannot reign where the living Christ is.

DEATH COULD NOT REIGN WHERE JESUS IS

Each time He confronted a dead body that body immediately lived, for death cannot reign where Jesus Christ is. The daughter of Jairus had just died, Jesus appeared at her bedside and the result was she rose from her bed alive. A funeral is passing through the gates of the village of Nain. A young man whose mother is a widow is walking after that coffin, sorrowing and pouring out her heart's grief. Jesus touches the bier, the procession is halted. Jesus Christ, the Lord of life, confronts the dead and the young man walks home from his own funeral. Why? Because no one can die or remain dead in the presence of the living Christ. Jesus Christ walked into a graveyard. He said "Expose the body of Lazarus". They rolled away the stone. Jesus Christ confronted the dead body of Lazarus and Lazarus arose from the dead. So Jesus Christ must die first.

Crucifixion was a slow death. Some victims lived for five days after having been crucified, so it was a slow death. Further down this chapter we read that Pilate was amazed that Christ was dead already. Christ must die or else these dying thieves will not die. Secondly, Christ must die if His word to one of those thieves is going to be fulfilled, for He said "This day thou shalt be with me in paradise." Please remember that the day of the Jew commenced in the evening, not at twelve midnight, but in the evening. It was coming now towards the evening. Jesus Christ must die in order that the dying thief must die the day that Jesus said "Today, thou shalt be with me in paradise".

TAKING DOWN CHRIST'S BODY

Now we need to note something from the Old Testament. If you turn back in your Bible to Deuteronomy 21, you will find there something about a body hanging on a tree. Verse 22 "And if a man have committed a sin worthy of death, and he be to be put to death, and thou hang him on a tree," please note that the Jews did not hang anybody to bring about their death. They hung the body up after it was dead and the Jewish way of killing is found in verse 21 "And all the men of his city shall stone him with stones, that he die." After his death his body is hung on a tree. "His body shall not remain all night upon the tree but thou shalt in any wise bury him that day (for he that is hanged is accursed of God;) that thy land be not defiled, which the Lord thy God giveth thee for an inheritance."

The apostle Paul tells us in Galatians 3:13 that Jesus Christ was accursed. "Christ hath redeemed us from the curse of the law being made a curse for us: for it is written, Cursed is everyone that hangeth on a tree". But it was impossible that Jesus Christ should hang on the tree during the night, because although Jesus Christ was cursed the curse had now passed, and instead of His body hanging on the tree to bring a curse upon the land His body must be buried because the curse has been buried already in His death. Christ was cursed as He hung upon that tree but when He died the curse was forever removed, in its great redemption purpose.

IMPOSSIBILITIES POSSIBLE

Firstly, it seemed singularly impossible that all these things would happen but they did happen.

They did not happen because angels came and took the body down and buried it. They did not happen because angels commanded the soldiers to do their bidding. No, but in the quietness of a providence that is wonderful and of a purpose so carefully mapped out from eternity by the infinite mind of a sovereign God, all these things work together into the Divine plan that all the Scriptures and the Word of God might stand in their integrity and infallibility.

Secondly, could I say, it seemed factually unlikely that this would happen.

There seems to be a complication here. His bones are not to be broken but He is to be pierced. That word "pierced" is "gashed". It is not a small pierce. It is not the piercing by the nails or the thorns. It is a gash. Of course that is quite evident when the Lord showed that gash to Thomas and He said "Reach hither your finger and you will be able to touch the piercing of my hands, it is only a little piercing, but you must thrust your hand into this terrible gash in My side." It seemed factually unlikely that His body would be preserved with not a bone broken but His side would be gashed in such a way.

Thirdly, it seemed particularly improbable.

Why do I say that? Because the soldiers at the cross were barbaric villains. They had gambled as the Saviour bore His load of sin and entered into the torments of the damned upon that cross for sinful humanity. Was it likely that they would have any respect for the body of the Son of God even though He was dead already? Was it not probable that they would rejoice in their barbarity and swing that iron bar against His legs to break them and blaspheme as they did it.

THE LINE OF THE CROSSES

Lastly, it was actually accomplished.

Some critic has said this could not be believed because the crosses were put up in a straight line. The way in which they broke the legs of their victims was this. Two men with a hand on each end of a huge iron bar swung it out and then across the legs of their victims. When they came with their iron bar they would surely have gone on to the other two.

But, you see it would be impossible for the crosses to be in a straight line, because then the dying thief could never have read the superscription above Christ's cross. The usual practice of the Romans was that the main victim was always set back from the others, so that they were crucified in a semicircle with the central cross and the main victim back from the line of the rest of the victims.

Now the dying thief blasphemed and cursed Christ with his companion and then suddenly there was a change. What brought the change? There is only one thing that brings a change in the hearts of men and it is the entrance of God's Word. "Where is He that is born King of the Jews?" was the first question of the New Testament. "This is Jesus, the King of the Jews." Read Matthew chapter one and you will find the emphasis on the name Jesus. Read Matthew chapter two and you will see the question "Where is He that is born King of the Jews".

In the providence of God that dying thief looked and he was able to see because of where his own cross stood. He could see clearly the superscription of the accusation. It is interesting to note that revisers were about even in the days when Pilate wrote his statement.

Pilate wrote the truth, directed not by a sinful heart but by the power of the Spirit, "This is Jesus the King of the Jews". The religious world came to him and said, "Write not, This is Jesus King of the Jews! Write that He claimed to be Jesus King of the Jews." But old Pilate believed in the Authorised Version. Do you know what he said? "What I have written I have written, it will not be changed."

The dying thief saw that he was being crucified with a King and he cried out "Remember me, Lord, remember me when Thou comest into thy kingdom."

Actually accomplished, it was Bishop Pearson who wrote, "These wicked soldiers found Christ dead. As barbarians they were enraged that they had no excuse to swing the bar and break His legs, for He was dead already. So in their anger, one of them took his spear and gashed it into the side of the Son of God's body, hanging on that cross. The wickedness of man was overruled by God to carry out this great establishment of the ratification of holy Scripture."

GLORIOUS FULFILMENTS

Let me bring you back to John 19 and you will see the distinct difference. The difference that one Scripture was fulfilled "and another scripture saith, They shall look on him whom they pierced".

Why was not a bone to be broken? Because Christ is the Passover Lamb. He is the antitype of all the 250,000 lambs that were slain in Egypt long ago at the first Passover and the millions of lambs that were slain down through the Mosaic economy and not one bone was to be broken. So He Who came to be our

Passover Lamb sacrificed for us, and not a bone of His body could be broken. But there is another Adam who was put to sleep in Eden's garden and his side was opened and out of his side came Eve, his bride. So the last Adam, the antitype of the first must have His side gashed, for only through that gash can come His bride, the Church of the firstborn ones whom He loved and having loved the Church He gave Himself for her.

There was another ark and Christ is our great Ark of safety. But there was another ark, an ark planned of God to bring Noah and his family and the animals safely through the deluge. It had a great door in its side. The only entrance to that ark was through that door. Jesus Christ must be pierced in His body in order that poor sinners can sing:

"Rock of Ages cleft for me,
Let me hide myself in Thee,
Let the water and the blood
From Thy riven side which flowed,
Be of sin the double cure.
Cleanse me from its guilt and power."

So here we have the Divine fulfilment. God has respect to His own Word. Nothing can ever alter it or take from it or add to it. His Word is sovereign, His Word is true, His Word is inherent, His Word is infallible, it is the Word of the God that cannot lie and the God that cannot die.

So the first thing we see is the ratification of Holy Scripture.

My time has gone, we will return to this subject in the new year by the grace of God.

AMEN AND AMEN!

The SEVENTH VEIL Christ rent at Calvary
the veil of His flesh

PART TWO

SCRIPTURE READING ~ JOHN 19:28-42

"After this, Jesus knowing that all things were now accomplished, that the scripture might be fulfilled, saith, I thirst. Now there was set a vessel full of vinegar: and they filled a spunge with vinegar, and put it upon hyssop, and put it to his mouth. When Jesus therefore had received the vinegar, he said, It is finished: and he bowed his head, and gave up the ghost. The Jews therefore, because it was the preparation, that the bodies should not remain upon the cross on the sabbath day, (for that sabbath day was an high day,) besought Pilate that their legs might be broken, and that they might be taken away. Then came the soldiers, and brake the legs of the first, and of the other which was crucified with him. But when they came to Jesus, and saw that he was dead already, they brake not his legs: But one of the soldiers with a spear pierced his side, and forthwith came there out blood and water. And he that saw it bare record, and his record is true: and he knoweth that he saith true, that ye might believe. For these things were done, that the scripture should be fulfilled, A bone of him shall not be broken. And again another scripture saith, They shall look on him whom they pierced. And after this Joseph of Arimathaea, being a disciple of Jesus, but secretly for fear of the Jews,

besought Pilate that he might take away the body of Jesus: and Pilate give him leave. He came therefore, and took the body of Jesus. And there came also Nicodemus, which at the first came to Jesus by night, and brought a mixture of myrrh and aloes, about an hundred pound weight. Then took they the body of Jesus, and wound it in linen clothes with the spices, as the manner of the Jews is to bury. Now in the place where he was crucified there was a garden; and in the garden a new sepulchre, wherein was never man yet laid. There laid they Jesus therefore because of the Jews' preparation day; for the sepulchre was night at hand."

Chapter 19 of John's Gospel and verses 34 and 35 "But one of these soldiers with a spear pierced his side, and forthwith came there out blood and water. And he that saw it bare record, and his record is true: and he knoweth that he saith true, that ye might believe".

The rending of the veils by Christ at Calvary. There are seven of them. There is the rending of the veil of darkness. There is the rending of the veil of separation between Himself and the dying thief. There is the rending of the veil of death by His conquering of death forever. There is the rending of the veil of the temple which was rent in twain from the top to the bottom. There is the rending of the veil of this earth with the mighty earthquake and the rocking of the whole earth on its axis. There is the rending of the veil of the graves when the graves were opened and the exhumed bodies were pushed forth with power to the mouths of every sepulchre around the Calvary area.

Now we come to something that took place as our Lord hung upon the cross, but only revealed after He was dead, the rending of the veil of His flesh.

THE RATIFICATION OF SCRIPTURE

I have already in a previous message dealt with the first point that I wished to underline, the ratification of the Scripture. You will have noticed that in verse 36 of this chapter these words are emphasised, "For these things were done that the scripture should be fulfilled, A bone of him shall not be broken. And again another scripture saith, They shall look on him whom they pierced".

We discovered that those two Scriptures refer, first of all, to the type of the Passover lamb in Exodus, where no bone of the lamb was to be broken, typifying

Christ our Passover Lamb who was sacrificed for us. The second Scripture has to deal with the prophecy of our Lord's return in the book of Zechariah when Israel, unbelieving and faithless, shall witness the second advent of Christ whose feet shall again stand in the mount from which He left. This same Jesus shall come again as you have seen Him go into heaven. That same Jesus will come again.

You can line up the modernists, you can line up the apostates, you can line up the infidels, they may be a great number and they may all say it cannot be and will not be but Jesus Christ shall come again and the Scriptures shall be fulfilled and every "i" will be dotted and every "t" shall be stroked.

We noticed some things in dwelling upon that first point - the ratification of Scripture. It seemed **singularly impossible** that this could happen. It was **factually unlikely** that it could happen. It was **particularly improbable** that it could happen, yet it was **actually accomplished**. It did happen as will all things written in this Book for this is not the book of man, this is the Book of the God that cannot die and cannot lie.

THE IDENTIFICATION OF THE SAVIOUR

We turn to the second point, the identification of the Saviour.

Jesus Christ must be identified as the Lamb of God. In the identifying of Him as the Lamb of God He must be the Son of God. The Gospel according to John is a most interesting Gospel.

If you read it you will find the constant repetition of the Word "witness". It is a Gospel of witness, a Gospel of testimony, a Gospel of record. The Greek word *martureo* is the word which is used in this Gospel. That word only occurs once in Matthew, only occurs twice in Luke but it occurs 33 times in the Gospel of John. If you study John's Gospel carefully you will find that there are seven witnesses. There is the witness of **the Father**, there is the witness of **the Son**, there is the witness of **the Holy Spirit**, there is the witness of **the written word**, there is the witness of the **works of Christ**, there is the witness of the **forerunner of Christ**, John the Baptist, and there is the witness of **Christ's own disciples**.

So there is a sevenfold witnessing to the fact that Jesus Christ is the Son of God, and Jesus Christ is the Lamb of God. Perhaps this afternoon you would care to read the first chapter of John's Gospel. You will find that John lifts his forefinger and he says "Behold the Lamb of God which taketh away the sin of the world." That chapter goes on to record the Lord's baptism. John said that he was given a special message from heaven that the person on whom the Spirit should alight and abide would be the Son of God. That, of course, took place at the baptism. There is the witness of John and you can look at the witness of the Father, the Son and the Holy Spirit and the written word and the works and His disciples. I commend you to find the 33 references to witnessing in this Gospel of John. Yes, indeed, the Lord Jesus Christ is marked as the Lamb of God.

THE PASSOVER LAMB

The final demonstration of this was at the cross. There are some things about the Passover lamb that are interesting to note.

The lamb had to be chosen. It was a chosen lamb. Christ was the chosen Lamb from before the foundation of the world. The lamb had to be pure, it had to be without blemish. The Lord Jesus Christ is a Lamb without blemish and without spot. He is the spotless, the stainless, the harmless, the sinless, the faultless, Lamb of God. If He be not that He cannot remove one of your sins, and He cannot shed blood valuable enough to cleanse the sins of your heart.

Further, the lamb had to be preserved for a period of 14 days so that it could be proved by scrutiny every day that it was without blemish. What was the scrutiny of Christ? For 30 years God's eye was upon Him and at the end of 30 years the voice from heaven said, "This is my beloved son in whom I am well pleased", There was no spot on Christ. His preservation was attested by heaven itself.

There is something else. **This lamb must be slaughtered in substitution**. A person could be pointed out and it could be said of that person, "the lamb died for you". That person was identifiable. Who was that person? It was the eldest, the firstborn son in every house.

Jesus Christ died as a substitute for all His people, but He died specifically as the substitution for an identifiable person. Who was that? Barabbas, Barabbas the murderer. Jesus Christ was nailed upon the cross on which Barabbas the murderer should have been nailed because this wonderful type is fulfilled to the last possible detail.

THE BLOOD PRESERVED

The blood of the Passover lamb did not run into the ground and be lost. The blood of the Passover lamb was caught carefully in a basin and into that basin was dipped the hyssop, and the sideposts and lintel of the door were struck with all that blood. Every drop of blood was struck onto the door so that every fibre of the wood of the door was stained right to its heart with that blood.

Under that crimson archway all people who would live have to go because there was no other shelter, no other security, no other refuge in the day when the judgment angel passed through Egypt, except under the crimson archway.

We often sing the hymn:

"When God of old the way of life
Would teach to all His own,
He placed them safe beyond the reach
Of death by blood alone".

Thank God all under that blood were beyond the reach of the fires of hell, were beyond the reach of the awful wrath of a sin-hating God, were beyond the reach of condemnation. Who is he that condemneth? It is Christ that died. Hallelujah for the blood of the Lamb! "It reaches me, it reaches me, pure, exhaustless, ever flowing, wondrous blood it reaches me."

You know what God is looking for today in your heart? He is not looking for your baptism certificate, He is not looking for your church membership or your Protestantism or your loyalty or any such thing, He is looking for the mark of His Son's blood. That is what He is looking for.

"When I see the blood." Does He see the blood on your heart today? Does He see that precious, precious blood of His well-beloved Son?

Let me turn to the last point I want to make in this message, the purification of the sinner.

The soldiers were ordered to break the Saviour's legs. This was a common occurrence to bring death quickly to those who were crucified. Crucifixion was a long, very long manner of dying. It could last three to four days, so in order to get rid of the victim they broke their legs. By breaking their legs instant death occurred. I have explained in a previous message how they came to the dying thieves first. Then they came to Christ and He was already dead. Now it did not give a qualm to these hardened soldiers of the Imperial Caesar to break the legs of the victims. In fact, they rather delighted in it. Stories of crucifixions tell us of the climax in the breaking of the legs of the victims. They came to this third victim and they could not break His legs to cause Him to die because He had already died.

THE RENDING OF HIS FLESH

So in his anger that soldier took a spear and plunged it with might into the body of Christ. You say, how do you know it was such a large gash? Because Christ said to Thomas "Take your hand and thrust it into my side" and He exposed to Thomas the spear gash in His side.

As one writer has said, "Done out of the satisfaction to kill Christ, the soldier delighted in mutilating His body." But something happened when that body was mutilated.

What does it say in the Scripture?, "Forthwith came there out blood and water."

That, of course, is a miracle. If you pierce the heart of a dead man there will be no blood and water flowing out, no matter how big is the gash you make. In fact, when death takes place the blood first of all congeals and then the two parts of the blood separate - the water and the blood. It is only after many hours that the blood liquifies again and if that happened and that blood was released, it would be water and blood that would come out. Notice the order in verse 34, it is very important, blood came first and then water.

CHRIST SHED HIS OWN BLOOD

Commentators and expositors agree on one thing and it is this, that Jesus Christ Himself must Himself, in a miraculous act, rent His own heart because it would be absolutely impossible for this to take place except the heart was first broken, and then the pericardium or sack around the heart contained the blood that flowed into it from that shedding. That, of course, is in keeping with what Christ said "I have power to lay it down and I have power to take it again".

What were the blood drops that Christ shed at circumcision? They were drawn from Him by the act of man.

What were the blood drops that fell from Him when He was scourged in Pilate's judgment hall? They were released from His body by the direct act of man in his hatred of the blessed Son of God.

What were those streams from the crown which pierced His brow? They too were brought from His body, drawn from it by a crown placed upon His head by the act of men and then beaten into His skull by the rod.

What were those streams that flowed from His hands and feet? Were they not taken from His body on that cross by the act of man?

But what of this, His heart's blood, His whole life?

He could have lost all that other blood drawn from Him by man and still have lived, but He was to die and He was to die by the shedding of His blood. "I have power to lay it down." When He cried "It is finished" He had already broken His heart and shed His blood within the veil for you and for me.

THE TWOFOLD FLOW

The blood of Christ is entirely different from the blood of any human being because it is the blood of the Incarnate Godman. When this blood flowed forth it flowed forth in a twofold way, blood first and then water. Why? Because the death of Christ does two things to the sinner.

It first of all cleanses the sinner from the penalty of his sins. That is the act of justification. "Justification is an act of God's free grace wherein He pardoneth all our sins and accepts us as righteous in His sight, only for the righteousness of Christ imputed to us and received by faith alone." The whole life of Christ. We were singing it this morning, " This is all my righteousness, nothing but the blood of Jesus." Cleansing from sin, pardon from sin was in that blood.

But there is another act, there is the act of sanctification.

Sanctification does not deal with the penalty of sin, sanctification deals with the power of sin. You need not only cleansing from the penalty of your sin, you need cleansing from the pollution of your sin. That is what the water is about. The cleansing water from the side of Christ emphasises that Jesus not only saves His people from the penalty of their sin but He saves them from its power. A saved man does not go back and walk in the ways of sin any more. "Christ breaks the power of cancelled sin, He sets the prisoner free, His blood can make ten thousand clean, His blood avails for me."

The man that tells you he is washed in the blood and goes back to his old life, never knew the power of the blood, but the man who says he is a new creature now hates the things he once loved, thank God and the things he once hated, thank God he now loves and you will know that that man has had the double cure, the water and the blood as is so sweetly said in Toplady's great hymn:

"Let the water and the blood
From Thy riven side which flowed,
Be of sin the double cure,
Cleanse me from its guilt and power.

Not the labour of my hands
Can fulfil Thy law's demands.
Could my zeal no respite know,
Could my tears for ever flow,
All for sin cannot atone
Thou must save and Thou alone"

PRECIOUS BLOOD

Oh how wonderful is that precious blood of Christ. Look with me at that riven side today and remember this, that spear thrust is a seal of prophecy. The Scriptures were fulfilled to their last dot and the stroke of their last "t". It was not only a seal of prophecy but it was a seal of shame. Christ must, even in death, bear upon Him the mark of the shame of sinful men for He did this thing for sinners.

"Twas you, my sin, my cruel sin,
His chief tormentors were.
Each of my crimes became a nail
And unbelief the spear.

It is also a seal of death. After that gash in Christ's side no one could say that Jesus never really died. I know a bunch of unbelieving agnostics have told us that Christ just swooned on the cross. Impossible! For His blood, every drop of it, had been drawn from His body. To what extent unbelievers go to try to deny the miracle of the death of the Son of God!

It is also the seal of purity, the water and the blood, and it is the seal of authority. This man who died on Calvary was the Godman, different from every other man, humanity and Deity in one Person with the blood of such infinite value and preciousness flowing in His veins that when it was shed it cancelled the debt of my sin forever and gave me a right to all the privileges of the sons of God.

"Precious, precious blood of Jesus,
Shed on Calvary,
Shed for rebels,
Shed for sinners
Shed for me."

CHRIST'S FOOTWORK

Could I finish with a thought that I mentioned in my opening prayer this morning. I was thinking about it in my study before I came to this service. Study the life of Christ and you will see His footwork. The great journey that He took out of eternity into time and all the journeys criss-crossing Samaria, Judea and Galilee, His footwork. Think of His handwork, the people that He touched and the healings He wrought. Think of His ear work. He always listened to the cries of those in need. When Bartimaeus cried the procession halted. There is only one thing that brings God the Son to a standstill, it is the cry of a sinner who wants His saving grace and cleansing power. Yes, we see His ear work and we see His lip work. Oh, what blessed words came from His lips. Never man spake like this man.

But today we are looking at **His heart work** and the writer to the Hebrews, Paul, tells us that this happened within the veil. Yonder in His heart, by an act of love for you and me, He broke His own heart and there was opened in the house of David a fountain for sin and for all uncleanness.

"There is a fountain filled with blood
Drawn from Emmanuel's veins
And sinners plunged beneath that flood
Lose all their guilty stains.

The dying thief rejoiced to see
That fountain in his day,
And there may you as vile as he
Wash all your sins away.

The other thief refused to see
That fountain in his day
And there may you, as vile as he
Throw your last chance away."

What is it going to be, faith in or rejection of Christ? You will answer that question now and it will be on the record of God.

AMEN AND AMEN

Appendix one
THE BLOOD AND WATER
by C.H. SPURGEON

TEXT ~ JOHN 19:34

"But one of the soldiers with a spear pierced his side, and forthwith came there out blood and water."

THIS LANCE-WOUND WAS THE SEAL OF DEATH UPON OUR LORD JESUS CHRIST. HIS ENEMIES WERE SO DETERMINED TO PUT HIM TO DEATH THAT THEY DRAGGED HIS LIFE OUT OF ITS PRINCIPAL ORGAN, AND THEN THEY pierced it, namely, the heart. It was not possible that Jesus Christ could have lived another moment longer, even had He been alive at that time; but when the heart was touched, death must come. Those who understand anatomy tell us that pericardium around the heart was pierced, and they say that from that there flowed the blood and the water; but I am extremely doubtful whether the pericardium in any state whatever could have yielded a sufficient quantity of lymph, for though there is water there, there is only a small quantity. In the state in which our Saviour was, blood and water might have been found naturally in his heart, but only in a very small and infinitesimal quantity. The fountain that flowed therefrom was miraculous, not natural but supernatural; or if natural, yet so exalted and so increased in quantity as to become in itself supernatural.

Certainly, however, the piercing of his heart was the indication to all mankind that "He was dead already". Now, little as that may seem in the eyes of those of you who do not love Him, it is a most important thing to those who trust Him;

for recollect, if Jesus Christ had not died, you and I must have perished. It was of no avail for our expiation that He sweat great drops of blood unless He had perfected the sacrifice. The law required life; if Christ had not laid down His life, the law would have required ours. In due time, our souls must have been cast into the second death on account of sin, if Jesus had not died, actually and truly died. But we are quite sure about it now, for His heart was pierced. Indeed, I may say that this is the one key-stone of the whole gospel system; for if Jesus did not die then we have no resurrection; for if He died not then He did not rise; and if we have no evidence of resurrection, the whole of our religion becomes a falsehood. But, brethren, He did die. His soul quitted His body. That corpse that was taken by Joseph of Arimathaea was as lifeless as any that was ever committed to the sepulchre; and He did rise again, in proof to us that we who die, and those we have parted with on the confines of this mortal life, who are, alas! all truly dead, shall certainly rise again, and in their flesh shall see God. This is a simple truth for you to hear, perhaps; but never did angel have such weighty news to tell as I have told you tonight, that God was made flesh; the very God that made heaven and earth took upon Himself our nature.

This heart-wound of Christ is also to be called The Source Of Purity. The text tells us that there issued from it a double flood of blood and water. We are not at a loss to explain this, because the apostle John, in his epistle, has told us that our Lord "came by water and blood; not by water only, but by water and blood," and he explains it by the connection that Christ came into the world by blood to take away the guilt of sin, and by water to take away the power of sin; by blood to remove the punishment, by water to remove the filth.

Now, dear friends, let us say that there is no blood and no water that can wash away sin anywhere but in Christ. All the blood of bullocks could not take away sin, though offered by Aaron himself, the father of the Levitical priesthood; and all the water in the world, though consecrated by bishops, and cardinals, and popes, cannot take away a single spot of iniquity. The only blood that can cleanse us from God's wrath is the blood of Jesus Christ Himself, and the only water that can wash out of us the damning stain of sin is the water which came from Jesus Christ's heart. If you want to be thus doubly washed, go to the Son of God for the washing. Go nowhere else, I pray you, for every other trust is but a delusion and a lie. Jesus Christ can put away the guilt of every sin. Though you have been a drunkard, an adulterer, a whoremonger, a thief, a murderer, yet the blood of Jesus Christ can wash you from the accumulated filth of years, and the water from

Christ's side can take away your propensities to sin, and change your nature, and make you holy instead of filthy, can make you pure in heart instead of polluted in spirit. Nothing else can do it. No lie was ever more extraordinary than the lie that baptismal water can regenerate the soul. I marvel more and more that I should find myself living in an age of such idiots, and have almost come to think that Carlyle was right when he spoke of our nation as "consisting of twenty million of people, mostly fools." So it seems to be, or else such a dogma as this would have been kicked out of the universe years since, and banished once and for ever to the limbo of lunacy as an outrage on common-sense. Is God the Holy Spirit confined to water, so that the priest's dropping it on the child's brow can work regeneration in the child's soul? Believe it not; it is a foul falsehood! But hold ye to this. That which alone can work regeneration is the water from the side of Christ, and when faith can get that, and trust that, the matter is done. Faith relies upon the sacred double flood; then the heart is renewed, the man is changed, the soul is saved by Jesus Christ.

Remember, too, that the water and the blood flowed from the same place, and flowed together; and, therefore, if a man would be saved, he must have the two. Tens of thousands would like to escape from hell, but they have no wish to escape from sin. Are there not multitudes who are very anxious to get rid of the punishment, but are not at all concerned to be delivered from the habit of iniquity? Oh, yes! the drunkard would fain be forgiven, but he would like to keep to his tippling. Yes, the lecherous man would fain have his constitution restored, and his iniquity blotted out; but he must go to his dens of infamy again. Such is not the religion of Christ. The religion of Christ demands of us that, if we take Christ, we should take him for the double purpose, to pardon for sins past, and to deliver from sins to come. I think it was Celsus, the ancient philosopher, who jeered at the great Christian advocates, saying, "Your Master, Christ, receives all the filth of the universe into His Church; He tells you to go about to find out thieves, drunkards, harlots, and such like, and to tell them to come to Him. Your religion is nothing better than a lazar-house, into which you thrust lepers." "Ay," said he who argued with him, "you have spoken well. We do receive them as into a lazar-house, but we heal them, sir, we heal them; and while into the one door the spiritually and morally blind, and halt, and maimed, and lame do come in as they are, the great Physician touches them with His grace, and cleanses them with the water and the blood, and they are not what they were any longer." Now am I addressing one man who feels that he is saved by faith, and yet he is sinning as he used to do? Give up that belief, sir, or it will ruin you. I pray you, do not indulge in it, for it is a delusion of Satan. Do I address one man who has a hope that perhaps he can so trust Christ as to be saved, and yet continue to live in his own wicked way! If anyone has told you that, he has told you falsely. Rest assured that you are mistaken. Christ never came to be the minister of sin. He came to save us, not in our sins, but from our sins. He will forgive us all manner of iniquities, but not if we love the iniquity, and continue in it; if you hug sin to your bosom, the viper will sting you; and no power, either human or divine, can extract the poison unless the viper itself be taken away. You must have both the water and the blood, and I pray that you may have both.

Appendix two
THE POWER OF THE BLOOD
by C.H. SPURGEON

TEXT ~ 1 JOHN 5:6

"Who is he that came by water and blood, even Jesus Christ; not by water only, but by water and blood. And it is the Spirit that beareth witness, because the Spirit is truth."

OH, THE POWER OF THE PRECIOUS BLOOD OF JESUS! DID YOU EVER FEEL IT, DEAR FRIEND? IF SO, YOU WILL NEVER DOUBT THE TRUTH OF THE ATONEMENT, FOR IT WILL BE VERY REAL TO YOU. NEVER CAN I FORGET the day when I first felt in my soul the power of the blood of Jesus. Christ's blood has the power to put away sin from the sight of the all-seeing Jehovah; but it also has the power, so far as man is concerned, to give peace to the troubled conscience, rest to the weary heart, joy to the miserable life. No one could ever have been more wretched and sad than I was when under a sense of sin, life had become almost unbearable though I was but a lad; but oh! what a leap my soul gave, from the very depths of despair up to the heights of overflowing joy, when I realised that Christ had come to me "not by water only, but by water and blood," and that He had put away my sins as far as the East is from the West, so that they should be remembered against me no more for ever!

"E'er since by faith I saw the stream
His flowing wounds supply,
Redeeming love has been my theme,
And shall be till I die."

Remember, my dear hearer, that Jesus Christ must come to you "by blood" or else He will never come to you "by water". Christ never gives a man holiness of life unless that man accepts Him as the great propitiation for sin. Do you ask, "How can Christ come to me by water and by blood?" The only way that I know is the one that I have pointed out to you over and over again; it is this. You are a sinner, lost and undone; Jesus Christ came to seek and to save the lost. To do this, He had to take the sinner's place, to bear the sinner's guilt, and to suffer the penalty that the sinner deserved to suffer. "He was wounded for our transgression, He was bruised for our iniquities: the chastisement of our peace was upon Him; and with His stripes we are healed." Have you faith enough to appropriate His work? Perhaps you question whether you may do so. Well, rest assured of this, there never was a sinner who trusted Christ, and then was told that he had no right to trust Him. Oh, no! He Himself said, "Him that cometh to me I will in no wise cast out," and He will not cast you out if you come unto Him. Can you believe that His blood was shed for you? Dare you rest your soul's salvation upon the great work of which He said, "It is finished," ere He bowed His head, and gave up the ghost? Will you now trust Christ as your Substitute and Saviour? You know those verses that we often sing -

"Just as I am - without one plea
But that thy blood was shed for me,
And that thou bidd'st me come to thee,
O Lamb of God, I come.

Just as I am - and waiting not
To rid my soul of one dark blot,
To thee, whose blood can cleanse each spot,
O Lamb of God, I come."

Is this the language of your heart? Then I venture to say that Christ has come to you, "not by water only, but by water and blood;" that Christ died for your sins according to the Scriptures, and that God will never punish you for your transgressions as Christ has borne the full penalty for them all. Then, if you have received Christ thus as coming to you by blood, I feel sure that you will also believe that He has come to you by water, to purify you from all defilement, and therefore you will not any longer knowingly and wilfully continue in sin. The gratitude which you must feel in your heart for all that Christ has done for you will constrain you to walk before Him in holiness and humility, and to seek to obey His will at all times.

Now, many of us are coming to the table of our Lord to commune with Him and with one another, and there we must specially think of how He came to us "not by water only, but by water and blood." The broken bread will remind us of His body broken for us, and the wine in the cup will bring to our remembrance His precious blood of the new covenant shed for us for the remission of our sins. Oh, what a wonder it is that we, who once were as the prodigal son in the far country, wasting our substance in riotous living, or perhaps even herding among the swine, are now welcomed at our Father's board among His happy forgiven children! A few years ago, nay, even a few months ago, some of us would not have been spending the Sabbath evening among the Lord's people in the house of prayer, and it would never have entered into our thoughts that we should be found sitting as honoured guests at His table. Our ideas of enjoyment then were very different from what they are now; the laughter of fools was then in our mouth, and perhaps the song of the drunkard issued from our lips. But now, by grace, a blessed change has been wrought in us, for we are washed, we are sanctified, we are justified in the name of the Lord Jesus, and by the Spirit of God.

0171 · 583 · 63 21

THE
❄ IAN R. K. PAISLEY LIBRARY ❄

OTHER BOOKS IN THIS SPECIAL SERIES

♦ **Christian Foundations**

♦ **An Exposition of the Epistle to the Romans**

♦ **The Garments of Christ**

♦ **Sermons on Special Occasions**

♦ **Expository Sermons**

♦ **A Text a Day keeps the Devil Away**

❄ AVAILABLE FROM ❄

AMBASSADOR PRODUCTIONS, LTD.

Providence House
16 Hillview Avenue,
Belfast, BT5 6JR
Telephone: 01232 658462

Emerald House
1 Chick Springs Road, Suite 102
Greenville, South Carolina, 29609
Telephone: 1 800 209 8570